Praise for
My Love,

"The right words at the right time can work wonders for our military families in these times of turmoil and change. Dianne Collier's *My Love, My Life* is perhaps the best book yet on military families and the unique challenges they face. Dianne offers wit, wisdom and authentic life lessons that ring true for anyone who has experienced the armed service. If you buy one book on military life this season, make it this one."

Celia Straus, author of *Prayers on My Pillow* and
The Mother Daughter Circle, Washington, DC

"An open and honest discussion from all aspects of the military. Dianne hits the pulse of the military life, from behind the scenes of the home front. A true '*Aide-Mémoir*' for any military spouse."

Lisa Hopkins, military spouse, Bosnia

"This is the most comprehensive effort attempted about the military life I have ever seen and it will be very well received by Canadians...this is the only way they will learn about our military families, and the effect deployments have on those at home."

Jane Snailham, author of *Eyewitnesses to Peace,* Halifax, NS

"The Canadian Armed Forces is not a job—it is a life. No one knows that better than Dianne Collier: she has spent all her adult life as a military spouse and a military secretary. Dianne has witnessed the good, the bad, and the ugly. The chapters dealing with support systems, a peaceful world, PMQs, and life after the military are particularly real and insightful. I would recommend this book to anyone."

John M. Clarke MMM CD, Chief Warrant Officer (Ret'd)
Former Base Chief Warrant Officer, CFB Petawawa/Force
Sergeant Major, Special Service Force, Petawawa, ON

"Dianne has captured the essence of the military spouse in *My Love, My Life* without being maudlin. The book is a great read and will be a welcome addition to many bookshelves around the world."

Margaret Hache, military spouse, Shelley, WA, Australia

"*My Love, My Life* is a rare find. A tribute to military spouses—a special look inside their hearts." [Excerpt from Foreword by]

Brigadier-General Peter J. Devlin
Commander of the Kabul Multi-National Brigade
Kabul, Afghanistan

"Your cover simply leapt off the screen and grabbed me by the throat! It's perfect! I love the title, and the picture speaks to my heart. It's a perfect example of 'You CAN tell a book by its cover.' The only thing I can say, Dianne, is you've done it again (I'm not surprised) and I think you may have outdone yourself. I can't wait to read it, and as always I am very proud of you. Thank you for letting me take a peek at your new baby."

Joanne Parent, Petawawa, ON

"Dianne has once again captured the life of today's military families. *My Love My Life* continues our story as told by a true Military Rose. Congratulations, Dianne."

Pat O'Keefe, military spouse, Edmonton, AB

"If you've ever wondered how military families survive in the turbulent world we live in, then look no further. Between the covers of this book, Dianne Collier takes the true-life stories of military family members—their hopes and dreams and sometimes nightmares—and magically weaves them into a rich tapestry that transcends national borders and illuminates the bittersweet life that military families live. From the triumphant joy of success achieved to the spiritual decimation of a lone, flag-draped casket on a rain-swept runway, the words pass quickly before the eye of the reader but somehow remain lodged deep within the chambers of the heart. And from time to time, a picture on the news or an article in the paper will trigger a resurrection of those feelings experienced and the words will return. Like the memory of the first flowers of spring, the fragrance remains, long after the blossoms are gone. *My Love,*

My Life, in the final tally, is much more than entertainment. It is a powerful and moving tribute to a group of men, women, and children who understand better than most that freedom is never free."

Colonel S. Arrington USAF, Inspector General,
Nellis Air Force Base, Nevada

"As a military wife knowing Dianne's unceasing efforts on behalf of the military community, I see this book as being a great success. She strives to cover all our issues thoughtfully and without bias. Hopefully, everyone will find something within *My Love, My Life* that they can relate to."

Amy Coxworth, military spouse, Petawawa, ON

"I have served over 34 years in uniform (the last 32 within the Regular Force) and have naturally seen many changes. The simplest of changes often brings with it unforeseen problems that frequently go undetected or are not spoken of for fear of upsetting the proverbial apple cart. Many of us rarely think of the effects all this change has on our families. Dianne Collier is a rare exception and her work in this book is a gentle reminder to all. The operational tempo and change over the past decade within the Canadian Forces have brought with them new challenges that each of our family members must cope with. Dianne's painstaking research and dedication will be appreciated by all who take the time to read *My Love, My Life*."

Lieutenant Colonel Robert McBride
Base Commander, CFB Petawawa

"Another excellent book from Dianne Collier that is certainly destined to become a resource material for military spouses. Anyone considering marriage to a military man or woman should consider this required reading, even those already in the Canadian Forces, because the emotions from "the other side" can be quite surprising. This book will help with the reality that it is the whole family that is involved in so many ways when one member is in the military. Well done, Dianne!"

Maj (Ret'd) T.J. Winchester, Kinkardine, ON

"*My Love, My Life* is such a welcome addition to our appreciation of the life of those who were highlighted in *Hurry Up and Wait*, as Dianne Collier's first collection published 10 years ago was entitled. This newest compilation of vignettes and commentaries of military spouses about their lives and their concerns is long overdue. Certainly, much has changed since 1994—both for the Canadian Forces and for members of military families. And yet, as *My Love, My Life* illustrates, for the partners and family members of personnel who wear the uniform and are scattered throughout the country and the world, their concerns, anxieties and delights are very much the same as those of an earlier generation.

Dianne Collier's collection is a testimony to the strength of those "left behind" and to the central importance of the family in supporting the mission of the CF [Canadian Forces]. It is also a testimony to Dianne Collier's determination to help create and sustain a sense of community among often isolated and anxious military families and to give voice to those who are often forgotten and rarely heard. This is a very fine book and we are all privileged that Dianne Collier continues to take the time and expend considerable energy in collecting stories and giving voice to those so frequently taken for granted."

Jane Errington, PhD., Professor of History,
Royal Military College of Canada, Kingston, ON

"If you read *Hurry Up and Wait*, then this book just gets even better. *My Love, My Life* is about the other Service—families. It is about those who love us, support us, and help us do our jobs to the best of our abilities. This is also a book about the experiences our families face because of their love and support for our professional endeavors. This is a must-read for anyone who wants to understand and learn about life as a spouse, partner, girlfriend, boyfriend, child or any member of a military family. To all the families who participated in this project, thank you and thank you, Dianne."

Lt (N) Mercy Yeboah, MSc.SS
Formation Social Work Officer, CFB Esquimalt, BC

"With her finger on the pulse of the Canadian Forces, Dianne Collier has again enriched our lives, recording so much truth and emotions from a collective group. This work should be a required-read—for everyone from a new entry service person to their spouses and families. Dianne has been the source of confirmation and acknowledgement for us all and has not wavered in her commitment to telling our story."

Leading Seaman (Ret'd) James R. Purcell, BA., Halifax, NS

"I met Dianne in 1997 when on a whim I called and asked for her help in sending balloons to a friend in the Canadian Army who was returning home from a deployment. I had never met her but had read her articles from an Army website. She helped me out then and continues to pour her heart and soul into addressing the needs of the families of military members deployed worldwide. Dianne is an asset not only to Canadian military families but to all who send their loved ones into harm's way. Her books continue to show the dedication of military families and the tremendous effort that goes into sustaining the military life. Thank you, Dianne!"

Major Marlene Kerchenski, United States Air Force Nurse Corp, Education and Training Programs Manager Bolling Air Force Base, Washington, DC

Dianne's new book *My Love, My Life* is a raw look at the life of the military spouse. I have lived in a military community for over 30 years, and reading the many accounts of the hardships, joys, disappointments and love certainly opened my eyes, heart and mind to the extended difficulties our military neighbors must endure. I encourage anyone even remotely associated with the military to read this book...you won't regret it!

Bob Sweet, Mayor, Town of Petawawa

My Love, My Life provides unique insight into the added responsibilities borne, and the anguish and sorrow often felt, by those whom our soldiers have left behind. The book demonstrates the need to recognize the sacrifices made by Canada's invisible regiment, the loved ones who keep the home fires burning.

Cheryl Gallant, Member of Parliament, Renfrew–Nipissing–Pembroke

My Love,
My Life

An Inside Look at the Lives of Those Who Love
and Support Our Military Men and Women

Dianne Collier

Published by

Box 424, Carp, Ontario
Canada K0A 1L0
(613) 831-3641
1-800-287-8610
info@creativebound.com
www.creativebound.com

ISBN 0-921165-83-8
© 2004 Dianne Collier

Managing editor:	Gail Baird
Text editor:	Holly Beanlands
Book designer:	Wendelina O'Keefe
Cover photo:	CP (JONATHAN HAYWARD)
Author photo:	Patricia Waters-Holst, www.theweddingspecialist.com

National Library of Canada Cataloguing in Publication Data

Collier, Dianne
    My love, my life : an inside look at those who love and support our
military men and women / Dianne Collier.

ISBN 0-921165-83-8

    1. Military spouses--Canada. 2. Military spouses--United States.
3. Military spouses--Great Britain. 4. Families of military personnel.
I. Title.

U773.C645 2004   355.1   C2004-900820-X

Dedication

To my grandchildren, Nicholas Collier and Lexie Collier, who bring such love and joy to my heart. Now we can play together.

To John, my husband of 37 years, who has always been there for me. Without his love and support and constant encouragement to me to do my own thing, I wouldn't have gained the confidence I needed to challenge myself and to follow a path that has brought me so much satisfaction. Now we can go fishing together.

To my sons and their wives, Chris and Leah, Trevor and Terry. You all have enriched my life so much and I thank God every day for blessing me with two sons I'm extremely proud of and two daughters-in-law that I love as my own. Now we can all enjoy your wonderful children together.

Acknowledgements

There are so many people I must thank that it's hard to know where to start. One of the greatest aspects of living the military lifestyle is the tremendous support that is available no matter where you turn, from friends, acquaintances, and even strangers. Such was the case when I started on this wonderful adventure. I thank each and every one of you who shared a story, shared some tears and who offered words of encouragement or assisted me in any way. Your faith in me to represent you well in this book touched my heart, and because you cared to share, others will benefit. I treasure each and every contact.

My travels to several military bases to conduct interviews provided wonderful opportunities, and sincere thanks go out to the following people for their tremendous hospitality:

Sue Fenton and BGen Ivan Fenton, Edmonton
Trish Stogran and Colonel Pat Stogran, Ottawa
Pat O'Keefe and Major Dan O'Keefe, Gagetown
Cindy Lentz and Sgt Darryl Lentz, Kingston

A special thanks also goes out to the following for their literary contributions:

Colonel Steve Arrington, USAF—"Military Spouses: There Is a Difference"
Leslie Doolittle—"American Woman"
Jacqueline Marcipont—"Home Fires"
Sue Bard—"On the Road Again"

This book would not have materialized without publisher Gail Baird's belief in my ability to tell our story. Gail took on this book with blind faith, and her listening ear and sound guidance were invaluable to me. Gail, you are a dear friend who has made a tremendous difference in my life and I thank you sincerely.

Wendy O'Keefe's talent to create a book cover that is exceptional is legendary. Having been overwhelmed with her design for the cover of my first book, I eagerly looked forward to her new vision and I certainly was not disappointed. Wendy, don't give up your day job, you are a talent!

Lindsay Pike was my steady contact at Creative Bound Inc., and out of a mountain of e-mails and telephone conversations, a friendship grew that I'm sure will only deepen as time goes on. Her encouragement at pivotal times drew me up by the bootstraps so that I could soldier on.

Special thanks must also go out to Celine Thompson, Director Military Family Services, and Commander (Ret'd) Heather Armstrong, Family Policy Team Leader, Quality of Life Directorate, for their assistance and support and to LCol J. Wall, Commanding Officer of 1 Combat Engineer Regiment, for his support of an Engineer wife, while I was in Edmonton.

Military Terms and Definitions

1 RCR	1st Battalion, The Royal Canadian Regiment
3's	trades training course
ADAPC*	Alcohol and Drug Abuse Prevention and Control Program
ASD	Alternate Service Delivery (services supplied by civilians)
ASU	Area Support Unit
BC*	Battery Commander
BDU*	Battle Dress Uniform
BiH*	Bosnia and Herzegovina
CF	Canadian Forces
CFB	Canadian Forces Base
Colt/Cav	a Combat Observation & Laser Team to find and designate targets. They use Bradley armored vehicles, Humvees, etc.
DH	"Darling Husband" "Damn Husband" (depending on the mood)
DND	Department of National Defence
E-4, E-5*	rank, pay level enlisted
EFMP*	Exceptional Family Member Program
HLTA	Home Leave Travel Allowance
HMCS	Her Majesty's Canadian Ship
ID	Identification
JLC	first step of a leadership course for Corporals
LTA	Leave travel allowance
LTC*	rank of Lieutenant Commander
MC*	Marine Corps

MFRC	Military Family Resource Centre
MS	rank of Master Seaman
MP	Military Police
NCM	non commissioned member
NDMC	National Defence Medical Centre
NOK	next of kin
OT	occupational transfer
PER	Personnel Evaluation Report
PLD	Public Liability Damage
PLDC*	Primary Leadership Development Course
PMO*	Project Management Office
PMQ	Permanent Married Quarters
PTSD	Post Traumatic Stress Disorder
QOL	Quality of Life
R & R	Rest and relaxation
RCR	Royal Canadian Regiment
Rear Party	Members of a unit who remain behind when personnel go on a tour—to attend to any administrative requirements for service member and to support the families.
SCAN	Second Career Assistance Network (to assist service members in preparing for life after the military)
SCONDVA	Standing Committee on National Defence & Veterans Affairs
Sgt	rank of Sergeant
SISIP	Service Income Security Insurance Plan
Spec Pay	Specialist Pay
TD	Temporary Duty
USAF*	United States Air Force
USN	United States Navy
Waivers	troops who have been on a foreign tour do not have to do another one for at least one year upon their return home— unless they sign a waiver enabling them to go sooner

* American Abbreviations

Foreword

My Love, My Life is a rare find: A tribute to military spouses—a special look inside their hearts.

The emotion of separation is complex. It tugs at our spirits and our feelings, in powerful and different ways for each of us. There is great concern both on the part of military spouses, for their loved ones serving away from home, and of those serving, towards their family and friends. The effect is real and touches people in different ways. For some, facing separation can be terribly upsetting and can leave them with a feeling of emptiness; for others, living through a separation can bring a sense of personal accomplishment. For most, it is an exercise in strengthening of character.

The Canadian military has invested a great deal of effort into improving the quality of life of the military family, including developing and running programs to give support to the spouses and families of soldiers that are deployed on operations, or away from home on course, tasking or exercise.

In recent years, we have seen what Dianne refers to as "the new breed of military spouse." We have lived through the past 10-plus years of Peace Support and Stabilization Operations, that have seen loved ones in places such as Bosnia, Croatia, Kosovo, East Timor, Haiti, Somalia, Afghanistan, Rwanda, the Persian Gulf and many other far away locations. Those who have not yet undergone a separation from their spouse will benefit from reading this book, which is rich in the experiences of those who have lived through that separation.

Some of the stories and comments in Dianne's book do not necessarily reflect the military's official stand on certain issues—nor do they have to. The experiences of each family are real, and these experiences colour each person's perception of life in the military family. Many military spouses need to, and should, connect with others who have similar or shared experiences. Through her book, Dianne has given people a means of connecting. The tremendous feedback she gets through her website provides clear evidence of the need for an outlet to express and share the concerns common to military spouses.

One of the most difficult emotional situations we deal with as a military community is the death of any of our soldiers. The loss of life is extremely difficult for both soldiers and their spouses to deal with. In the course of our mission in Afghanistan, Operation ATHENA, we lost two soldiers as a result of a mine-strike. At that time, I was reminded of just how much people require each other's support. This is true not only for the Canadian Forces, but also for the military forces of other nations. During the repatriation ceremony at the airport in Kabul, Afghanistan, as the caskets of two young men were moved to the aircraft, soldiers from 25 nations lined the tarmac, to show their respect and support to their brothers in arms. This act demonstrated how much events like this affect even soldiers from other nations. In the days following this tragic event, I came to realize that the Canadian Forces deserves much credit for the programs it has put into place to provide support to both the military members and the military families in their time of need. Many of the programs, involving group-support from the other members of the military family, are working extremely well. It is in times of crisis like this that I look at how we deal with these situations and I am extremely proud to be a member of our Canadian Forces.

Dianne's book is special. It provides inspiration and understanding. I hope that you will enjoy reading and reflecting on the powerful words in *My Love, My Life*. Members of the Canadian Forces are blessed to be able to draw on the great strength of our spouses, families and friends.

> Brigadier-General Peter J. Devlin
> Commander of the Kabul Multi-National Brigade
> Kabul, Afghanistan
> January 2004

My Love, My Life

Introduction

When I first started thinking about writing another book on the military lifestyle from the spouses' point of view, I thought it would be an easy book to write. Having already been through the book-writing experience a couple of times and knowing the process, I expected this book would just fall into place. What I found was just the opposite. In the 10 years since my research on this subject for my first book, *Hurry Up and Wait: An Inside Look at Life as a Canadian Military Wife*, so much has changed.

I've now retired from working for the military, and great strides have been made by DND to catch up with the times. And so, I felt *My Love, My Life* was a timely book—to see just how much had changed. I also realized that since I am no longer part of the lifestyle, my up-to-date knowledge of changes within the lifestyle might not be accurate, and so my research took on a more intense direction. However, with the wonderful support of e-mail, I have been in touch with many military spouses, and as one lady said to me: "Dianne, don't talk to us, talk *for* us." And that is what I have done.

As with any book, it is impossible to cover all issues, but what is written within these pages is what you spouses have told me is important to you. Everyone won't relate to all that is included, but each one of you will relate to some sections of this book. It is my hope that those who read *My Love, My Life* will come away with a new appreciation and understanding for those who keep the home fires burning.

After the release of my first book in 1994, I had the opportunity to travel and speak with military families all across Canada and in Europe. Those wonderful meetings started me on a path I still travel to this day—supporting military spouses at every opportunity. At last count, I have visited over 28 of our Military Family Resource Centres (MFRCs) and spoken to a variety of groups, from military wives to MFRC staff and board of directors, to civilian groups and organizations, and to school children of all ages.

I've heard countless stories pertaining to the military lifestyle—many from people in general conversation who probably didn't realize that even they were sharing so much of their own experiences with me. No matter what country our partners serve, military spouses are universal—we all share the same emotions in this challenging lifestyle. And so, throughout this book you will find stories and comments from Canadian, American and British spouses.

Over the ensuing years I've tried to find ways to unite military spouses; to show them that they are not alone in all the emotions they experience and that these emotions are common to the lifestyle; and to show them how they can support each other. With families most often living thousands of miles away, the support between military spouses is very important.

One of my initiatives was to create a website dedicated to military wives. Salute to Supporters (http://www.renc.igs.net/~tcollier/), a place where military spouses can feel at home, was created in April 1999, and you will find it referred to throughout this book. The response to this website has been tremendously positive, and through it I have met so many interesting, supportive people. We've laughed together and we've cried together. Friendships have been formed and a sense of belonging has taken hold.

However, I have taken some criticism for specifying I was supporting military *wives* as some felt that I was not keeping up with the times and that I should include men whose wives were in the military, but life as a military wife is what I know and this group is by far the biggest and has the largest history in the lifestyle. With other projects I was involved in to continue my support, the role of stay-at-home husbands and fathers has surfaced time and time again. Their numbers have certainly increased in the military lifestyle these last few years and I have included comments on their role in the book.

Since the website's early days, I have received hundreds and hundreds of e-mails from military spouses everywhere and I answer every message I receive. At times it has been overwhelming. But what all of this has shown me is just how much of a need there is for military spouses to not only connect with each other but to be supportive. I've also seen just how utterly alone and isolated they quite often feel.

When I gave thought to producing another book dedicated to military spouses, I felt a strong need to include some of the e-mails that have been sent to me. I spent a considerable amount of time giving thought to how the senders of these e-mails would feel about seeing their thoughts, comments and concerns published in this book, and in the end, I decided that what they had to say was important and should be included. However, I never betray a confidence and have taken great pains to change the identity and locations of those who shared their thoughts and feelings with me. And so, I hope that any of you special people who might recognize your comments in print will find comfort in the fact that I found your thoughts worth sharing because they will help someone else in this lifestyle feel just a little better and less alone. I look on these personal testimonials as another way in which military spouses are supporting each other—anonymously.

Since I retired from my full-time job in March 2001 as a Commanding Officer's secretary at an infantry battalion, and with my husband's retirement from the military in 1992, I am no longer part of the military lifestyle. But, I wanted to ensure that the direction I was following with this book was the right one. This is not *my* story, but the thoughts, worries and experiences of today's military spouses, and so I needed to ensure that what I was doing in representing them in this book was what was important to them.

I designed a fairly straightforward questionnaire, which was distributed at every opportunity—by e-mail, through personal contacts, at all speaking opportunities I participated in, and by regular mail. It was just amazing how the spouses' network embraced my request to help spread the word about my new book and questionnaire, and it wasn't long before I was receiving requests for questionnaires. However, after learning that spouses had been showered with various questionnaires through the resource centres and through the Department of National Defence in the last while, my hopes were not to break any records with a large return but to receive enough of a response to give me an indication of whether I was going in the right direction with this book. And you have told me I am. I thank you all sincerely for completing the questionnaires and throughout the book you will find references made to the comments you provided in them.

I have found many differences between the survey results of today's questionnaires and the questionnaires released in 1992 for *Hurry Up and Wait*. At that time, very few ladies identified themselves on the questionnaire. Many were very skeptical of what I was doing and unsure of who I was, and they were nervous about revealing their identity. Was it fear of the unknown? Fear of how their thoughts might affect their partner's career? Probably a little of both. But I must tell you that today, the questionnaires that I have received—

with the exception of a half dozen responses—ALL contained names and addresses. Military wives are no longer afraid to speak their mind. I thank you all sincerely for that.

My Love, My Life is an inside look at the challenging world of those who love and support our military. Today's military spouse faces many challenges during very difficult times. Gone are the days of complacency, two- and three-year tours to Germany where we were able to travel around Europe, completely at ease.

The entire atmosphere within the military community has changed drastically in the last 10 years. Doing more with less has become the norm by which our partners must work, and the worry and stress level of our families have increased tenfold as our service members depart to wartorn countries.

Not since the Korean War has there been so much fear of the unknown to deal with. However, all is not as bleak as it might sound. The Department of National Defence has made great strides since the 1980s in acknowledging the role spouses play in this challenging lifestyle, and offers various forms of support. *My Love, My Life* discusses some of the support available. Only you can decide if there is enough.

My Love, My Life delves into the hearts of our spouses—what they think, how they feel and who they really are. Personal stories will give you readers a glimpse of the emotional turmoil we face day in, day out. The pride in what our partners do and how they positively represent our country is just as strong as ever, but for some, the willingness to accept the challenges of today's military lifestyle is lacking. This book will look at the new breed of military spouses, to understand where they are coming from and why, and to note how their refusal to accept the military lifestyle is affecting our service members.

In presenting many of the stories you'll find in *My Love, My Life,* I've recorded them as they were told to me. While my own personal opinion is not always reflected in the comments of some of the participants, what is important is that their stories and their concerns are very real to them. As a military wife who has also worked for the military, I have a keen understanding of some of the difficulties facing those professionals who specialize in dealing with military family issues.

In *My Love, My Life,* I've included comments from military wives (those who live the military lifestyle as well as those who have chosen not to), men whose wives are in the military, and girlfriends because they have special issues relating to this lifestyle, and I quite often hear from them. I want their worries and concerns represented.

In putting this book together, I found there was so much that *should* be included that deciding what to include and what to leave out was a definite challenge. One book alone cannot cover this ever-changing lifestyle, but my hope is that *My Love, My Life* will give you some insight into what life is really like for those who follow their hearts. You will find tears and laughter as men and women from different nationalities and backgrounds come together to live in a lifestyle that offers many, many challenges. This book is their story—laughter, tears, warts and all.

Chapter 1

The Supportive Military Family

I love the life. I hate it. I'm sometimes
ambivalent...but I love my husband dearly and
at the end of the day, that is all that counts.

Today, more than ever before, guys and gals create a mental picture of the perfect mate. Many women have a checklist for scoring a potential husband. In my day, I suppose we had the same thing although it wasn't so blatant or prominent in our lives. We just quietly assessed and accepted or rejected. Marrying a military man wasn't in my imaginary picture at all. Neither was a man with tattoos or dirt under his fingernails. Little did I know that I would indeed marry a military man, with a tattoo, and the dirt under his fingernails that is normal for a field engineer.

Education wasn't a high priority then—at least not in my circle of friends— and looking for a rich partner was considered by some to be a very selfish approach to marriage. It was more or less the luck of the draw if you ended up with a partner who had pockets full of money. What was important then and still is today is that, besides the emotional connection, he be faithful, honest and hard-working, and a good family man. I always joke that I married my husband for his money, and after 37 years of marriage I'm still trying to find it.

Many young women who are in a somewhat serious relationship with a member of the Armed Forces are researching the lifestyle before they commit. They want to know just what they are getting into, what will be expected of them, and they want to know if they can handle all the challenges they will be faced with. The "I love you and will follow you anywhere" mentality has been replaced by some with "I love you and will follow you anywhere—maybe."

This isn't a self-centered approach; it's a practical one. Women want to learn all they can about the military lifestyle because it is so foreign to them. They should be prepared to have not only the strong love they feel for their boyfriend, but also the ability to adjust to a life filled with long absences and loneliness, coupled with a necessarily strong sense of independence. They are wise to investigate and to consider the particular lifestyle demands put upon a military spouse before committing to undertake that lifestyle.

Since my website was put on-line, I have been flooded with requests for information on the lifestyle, and the question I get asked the most is, "What is it like to be a military wife?" In fact, as I write this section of the book, I've been asked to speak to a local church group answering this same question—in half an hour. How do you send an e-mail or speak to a group and explain all the emotions you go through in this lifestyle? How do you help civilians understand how our lives are different from theirs? It's a huge task to perform in a short amount of time within the confines of e-mail. What you really need is a one-on-one meeting where questions can be immediately answered and these young ladies can be given a balanced account of the pros and cons of living the military lifestyle. I've often thought some wives whose husbands have been in the military for 20 to 25 years or are retired from the lifestyle would welcome an opportunity to mix and mingle with our young girlfriends and wives of today. There is so much that could be learned from them. A great idea would be for any ladies' group to invite these older, more experienced wives to a coffee morning. Let them mix and mingle. I guarantee it would be a morning well spent.

I take the question of what it is like to be a military wife very seriously and do my best to answer it honestly, bearing in mind that I certainly don't want to be the one who might sway some young lady from committing to her boyfriend and the military lifestyle. You create your own life when you marry a military man. You make the best of where you live—you bloom where you are planted. No two people will find this lifestyle the same—some will take on the challenge with gusto while others will creep into it, unsure and somewhat overwhelmed.

Besides the girlfriends and wives that comprise the majority of the supporters in this challenging lifestyle, are the many men now faced with the role of supporter. They remain home while their partners go off to fulfill their military duties. These men are a kind of pioneers in that they are not only carrying out a role new to them, but having to deal with a system that in general is geared towards wives who play the supportive role; now the system must make way and acknowledge the role of stay-at-home husbands. As with anything else that is new and different, it will take time to integrate the requirements of male spouses into the current system of support.

This chapter takes a look at those who love and support—whether they be girlfriends, wives or husbands—and shows some of the unique challenges each group faces.

Girlfriends

I was a little surprised at the large number of girlfriends who contacted me— and still do. They consider themselves to be part of the lifestyle but find that often both military wives and the system don't acknowledge them and so they feel left out. Many are in much shorter relationships than common-law spouses, have no legal standing, and when their partner goes on tour, don't know where they stand, where they fit in. They feel they are on the outside looking in and they want more than that because they feel they are part of the 'family' too. And so they look for help wherever they can find it. The following stories give you a good indication of some of the problems these ladies are dealing with.

Your website has been heaven sent in a very hard time for me. Thank God for the Internet! I'm currently engaged to a pilot who is in language training in Quebec and going to Manitoba at the end of November to start flight training. I know nothing about what's going on in his life, I know nothing about military policy and procedures, and I'm totally confused.

Being a pilot in the military has been a dream of Kevin's for a long time. He comes from an aviation background; his father is a helicopter pilot (civilian). We got engaged in December and he left for boot camp at the end of January. I'm still living in British Columbia. We visit each other every 6 to 7 weeks but I still have no idea what's in store for us in the future.

We never talk about it, because I had a very hard time dealing with the whole apart thing, and the military in general. Now that I'm used to the apart thing, I still have no idea about the military. I feel that I need to know what is going to happen to me when I leave my very comfortable environment and join him at a base somewhere. I need to know if this is a life for me. I have so many questions and no one to answer them. I get bits and pieces from Kevin; he doesn't volunteer the information because he knows my feelings about the whole situation. I'm willing to accept a change if I can get my questions answered. And, he doesn't think that he should add stress to my life by telling me stuff. Stupid huh? Is there anywhere that I can go to talk to someone, get something to read, anything that would help me plan for the future that we're supposed to start together?

I'm sure I sound like a very confused individual, but like I said, we don't communicate on this subject and I think it's time that I found out some information. What is the life of a military wife like?

As I read this plea for help, I could easily place myself in this lady's shoes. The fear of the unknown is often worse than dealing with "whatever." The first thing that jumped out at me when I finished reading her message was "communication." She and Kevin are not communicating, and at some point they are going to have to. The fact that communication isn't there at this point in their relationship doesn't bode well for their future together in the military lifestyle because trust and communication are two "must-haves" if you are to succeed in your relationship—whatever the lifestyle. Granted, he is no doubt extremely busy with his training, but that's always going to be the case. He, like all his peers, will just have to find time to be there for his partner as often as he can.

It takes more than love to survive the military lifestyle, and the wise military man is one who acknowledges and understands the difficulties his partner will have sharing this lifestyle with him. He will do all that he can to answer her questions and alleviate her fears—putting it off because it's a touchy subject is definitely not the way to go.

I am currently a military girlfriend en route to being a military wife. My boyfriend has been overseas for the past year. In our two-year relationship we have spent a year and a half apart and survived. I have been questioning if the military lifestyle is for me. Your stories give me some things to think about. I had assumed that the lives you described raising children on your own, many nights and days of loneliness, etc., were what I had in store for me. Many have asked me, 'Is it worth it?' I am not sure.

Because they are so new to the world of military families and the military in general, ladies quite often ask me questions that really show just how the fear of the unknown can add to their stress level:

I first want to say thank you for having a site that deals with dating someone in the military and not necessarily being a spouse of a military man. I am writing you because I have a few questions and I am hoping that either you can answer them or point me in the right direction. My boyfriend is graduating from basic training in a week. He just found out that he will be stationed in Hawaii. That is all the information I have on the situation, but I am planning on going and visiting him in a month. The problem is that I do not know if I can stay with him or if I need to rent a hotel room. I do not know what island he will be on or where the base is. He will get me that information as soon as he knows, but the sooner I can order the plane tickets the cheaper they are and I don't have money to throw around. I am also wondering if I need ID to get onto the base. He is on active duty for the next four years and I want to make sure that he is able to have visitors as well as be able to pick me up from the airport on a Sunday. I would be very happy if you could answer any of these questions or let me know who I can talk to about these questions.   —Desperate

My boyfriend was just posted to Petawawa a month ago. I am not living there right now but I am looking for a job in the area and am living back at home in Thunder Bay. As part of my schooling, I have to do a placement in June so I am going to try and do my placement either on the base or at Atomic Energy [of Canada Ltd.]. The only problem is that I find that there are very few jobs for university-educated women around there. I feel like if I want a career in human resources that I have to move to Ottawa. Do you know if a lot of women live in other cities because they cannot find work there? I feel like if I stay there, I am doomed to becoming a stay-at-home wife (which is not a problem) but I want to use my five years of education..."

What a wonderful website. My boyfriend or, well, 'friend' at the moment, is on the HMCS [Her Majesty's Canadian Ship] Regina, and leaving in two weeks for seven months. I did not get any information to prepare me for the changes that were to happen. We were not together long, and had distance to deal with (five hours if I take the bus). But we were making it work, and were both really happy, and had talked a bit about his trip. We had agreed that we would be together, keep in contact via e-mail and some phone calls while he was gone. When he returns I will be living in Victoria, and that will help us. I will be finished college, and moving for better work opportunities. Also we will be able to see each other more often.

I found that as he would say more or find out more about his deployment that he became more and more distant, and that's where our relationship changed, and when he decided that he did not want us to be together, but just friends. He seems to be very confused and will contradict things that he has said earlier, and what he does say is a little different every time. He has said that he may like us to try our relationship again when he returns, but has also told me not to wait for him.

The hardest part even now, where we are just friends, is the lack of information that I get and resources that I have access to. Also the lack of knowledge that I have on what he goes through to prepare for the trip. I find it very hard to understand the life he leads, and that I was to be a part of. It is like a foreign language, with its own rules.

I just feel like there is so little support for someone like me. I am finding it very hard not knowing what he is going through, and not knowing how to deal with anything or how to talk to him about it. I know that I have to accept his decision to be nothing more than friends, but it's hard to watch someone you love change so much so fast, and not be able to understand it all.

This young lady and I exchanged one or two more e-mails before she moved to Victoria. When I reconnected with her nine months later, sadly their relationship hadn't worked out and they were no longer seeing each other.

In the beginning I never thought I would make it. I am a girlfriend of a West Point Cadet. When my boyfriend of three years left I was absolutely crushed. Time went by slowly and I went to school and we went almost four months not seeing each other. There were days I never thought I would ever make it, but I have so far. Though the first year is getting closer to an end I still have three more years of this craziness. But it has been thanks to my sorority sister Margaret, who is also an army girlfriend. Her boyfriend will be leaving in two weeks to serve six months overseas. I just want to thank you for having this website. It really means a lot to me to hear others' stories, when I can relate so well. This has been the hardest year of my 20 years of life, but with hope and love Jim and I will make it through, and we take it one day at a time!

One of the most common factors in all the messages I've received from girl-friends was their frustration over not understanding what the military lifestyle was all about and the need to know how to survive long separations and still keep the relationship intact:

I'm one of those Navy girlfriends you were talking about on your web page. My boyfriend, Charles, is away at fleet school on the east coast. We have been together for six months now and although I love him so much and would never even consider leaving him—it is so hard to have him away. Our other friends (the men are in the military and their relationships are about as new as ours) are getting engaged and have not yet suffered a long separation. They help me out a lot but I could still use some advice from someone who has experienced this separation. Charles is only away for three months now, but it seems like forever. Now I have just found out that the ship he is stationed on when he gets out of school is confirmed for doing the Gulf tour next year. That is a six-month trip! He and I are very much in love and do plan on getting married someday so this is something I know I will have to live with for the rest of my life. It's kinda scary. Thanks.

Hi to all you ladies who have loved ones away. I know how every-one feels because I am going through the same thing as everyone else. It's really hard when you move into a new city and your fiancé has to go overseas and you don't know anyone. To make matters worse, you don't get any support from the military because you're not a wife. I don't think I will ever understand the way the military works. You all take care and stick together as one. I am really lonely because I don't know anyone up here (Halifax). I came from a small town in Newfoundland. So that makes it even harder for me to get out and meet people. Thanks for listening.

When the man you love is serving overseas in a territory such as Kosovo, it is all you can do to not drive yourself insane. Even though

*we are not married, I have faith in him and that my prayers guide him at night
for the next four months as he serves at Camp Bondsteel. This is his second
time there and hopefully he will be getting leave soon. Wish on a penny I guess
you could say.*

One of the first things a member new to the Canadian Forces must do is
sign a Next of Kin form. This is kept in his personnel file, and should there
ever be an accident or death, the person listed as next of kin is the first to be
notified by the military. When a serviceman marries or even enters into a committed relationship, unless he has that Next of Kin (NOK) form changed to
designate his partner, she will not be the first point of notification. I've
received several messages from wives or girlfriends who have been hurt
because their partner's parents were the first to be notified when an accident
occurred. And sometimes, when there are strained relationships within the
family, the stress of a serious situation with the service member is magnified if
the military hasn't notified the proper person first. The military itself gets
blamed when, in fact, they are just following standard procedures by notifying
whomever is listed on the Next of Kin form. The onus is on the serviceman to
ensure that his personnel records are kept up to date.

*My fiancé left for boot camp two weeks ago today. It is so hard hav-
ing him gone and the worst part is not knowing anything about what
is going on with him. During the first week of boot camp he had to go into the
hospital because they thought that he was having a heart attack, and because
we aren't married yet, they contacted his mother instead of me. We have lived
together for the past three years, but they preferred to contact his mother who
he hasn't lived with in about six years. To me this just doesn't seem right. I am
so lonely without him here. The time goes so slowly. He won't be home for
another four months, and then we are getting married. Hopefully that will
make the situation better because after we get married he has to go to
Germany for two years. It makes me feel so much better to know that there are
other people going through a similar situation.*

Surprisingly, many girlfriends have the idea that they can't access their local
Military Family Resource Centre (MFRC) because they are not married to
their partners.

Thank you. Thank you. I almost cried when I found this page [Girlfriends] on my website. My boyfriend, who I live with, is going to the Gulf for six months. It has been one month already and it is VERY lonely. I feel very isolated, as I am not connected in any legal way to him, and am not able to access the resources out there for military spouses. We are going through a lot right now, the least of which is trying to save money to go and meet each other in Europe in late May for his leave. As we are not married, I am not eligible for HLTA [Home Leave Travel Allowance]. It is nice to find a page for my unique situation and I am wondering if you know of any chat or support groups available for girlfriends of CF [Canadian Forces] members on deployment?

When I responded to her message I asked her why she couldn't access her local MFRC.

I got home feeling particularly down today, and found your letter. It really lifted my spirits. I guess what I meant when I said that I was not able to access the resource centre is that I kind of feel like people will not take me seriously, as all the programs and resources are geared toward spouses. I guess I just feel like I don't belong in a group of wives yet. Maybe I am just being too nervous and must need to reach out.

It's pretty scary to think about marrying into this life, but when you love someone, you just do what you have to do I guess. It just makes me sad to think of being alone for half of the next 20 or so years. How do you cope? Half of our relationship has been spent apart. How do you know if it's good, if you're always apart? I find it so hard when he comes home, because I miss him so much when he is gone, but when I see him again, it's always like we are strangers a little bit. Does this ever get easier?

She and I corresponded for several months and I shared her excitement as she headed off to Europe for that much-anticipated meeting with her boyfriend. Unfortunately, things didn't go well and the last I heard from her, they had decided to go their separate ways and she was remaining in Europe to do a bit of traveling.

• • •

The Internet has made a considerable difference in the lives of military families. They can communicate by e-mail with their loved ones while they are away and they can also join many on-line groups established to support those in the military lifestyle. Several military spouses have also created their own websites offering support. But for some ladies, they are more restricted than others in sharing their thoughts and concerns. For example, Navy wives can't discuss the location of their husband's ships (quite often they don't even know where they are). And what about those ladies whose partners are in a confidential trade like special operations or intelligence? These ladies feel that they suffer more loneliness that most:

Oh my God I feel like I've been saved! I've just found your website. I'm five months into this lifestyle and clueless. I don't understand the lingo; my boyfriend is with a unit that I can't even talk about (special operations) which makes it 10 times worse. He's in Afghanistan now. I don't know where to look for support. I have found a military wives' page, and they are all very nice ladies, but they all have children and have been with their mates for so long, I have a hard time feeling like I can fit in. Not to mention they all talk about which area their husbands are in and again, I cannot. ANY information you can give me regarding this lifestyle would be welcomed with open arms and heart.

Some ladies see their transition from girlfriend to wife in a positive light and hope that with their new 'title' will come a better understanding of the lifestyle they have committed to living:

It's nice to see that there is finally a site for the girlfriends. My fiancé is currently in Bosnia. Three years ago he also served in Bosnia. At that time we had already been together for three years. On that tour I felt like I was in a world of my own, like no one around me understood how I felt or what it was like. There was no support from base since we were not married. I didn't know about the newsletters, coffee breaks or the evening outings. On this tour, however, I get to experience both sides of the fence. During the first three months I will be a fiancée/girlfriend and for the remainder of the tour I will be a wife. Whether you are common-law or a girlfriend, remember that you are not alone. There are more of us out there.

From my own experiences of working for an infantry unit that went on several six-month tours, I do know that the unit creates a mailing list before the tour to use in sending out newsletters. In addition, they also create fill-in-the-blank forms for each unit member to complete and return to the Rear Party notifying them as to whom they want to receive the newsletter. Many times a unit would send newsletters not only to a member's wife, but also to his mother. In fact, if the member's partner was not going to be at her normal residence address for the duration of the tour, then her address during that time could be inserted on the newsletter form and the unit would ensure the newsletter was sent to her. Again, the onus is on the service member to ensure that the unit's rear party receives the correct information before he departs.

To sum up this section on girlfriends, I feel that these special ladies need more support and understanding. While some might eventually separate from their boyfriends, many will go on to become military wives. Not only do they need to feel more welcome at our Military Family Resource Centres, but they also need to be embraced by military wives and made to feel welcome. They need and deserve more support from their partners as well, to ensure that their well-being is looked after while the military member is absent. The members can accomplish this by giving serious thought to whose name should be provided as the primary person to be notified on the next-of-kin form; if they decide that this should be their mother rather than their girlfriend or wife, then it should definitely be discussed with their partner BEFORE they leave on tasking. Given the emotional turmoil that an accident or death can take, it is very important to make sure the appropriate person is listed on the NOK form and that family members and partners are aware of who that person is. Ensuring that this information is up-to-date can go a long way to alleviating a stressful situation.

To all the girlfriends reading this chapter, I hope I have represented your thoughts and concerns well and shared what is important to you. I hope that all girlfriends will find many answers to their questions throughout *My Love, My Life*. You are just as much a part of the lifestyle as any of us, so hang in there and keep smiling.

And now, I'll leave you all with a little chuckle provided by another special girlfriend:

I have a lot of time on my hands while my boyfriend is away in Bosnia. I am a bit younger than all the military wives and it's really hard to find someone to talk to that knows what I'm going through, to share some little stories with or just to have a shoulder to cry on.

A funny incident just happened to me: In all my infinite wisdom in care package making, I decided to make his favorite squares just to show him that I loved him. I wrapped them up and, not thinking, I put a few pieces of bread with them so that, if any air got in, they wouldn't dry out. Anyway, six weeks later, and after I came to my senses and had informed him not to eat them, my package arrived. As I had already guessed, the bread had started to sprout. Poor Dwayne, being so homesick and flattered that I baked them just for him, decided to eat them. He said they were fine but after six weeks in with moldy bread, I don't really think they were meant for human consumption. Anyway, I thought it was pretty funny in a gross sort of way. It just proved how home-sick he really was....

Wives Who Don't Live the Military Lifestyle

More and more military wives are deciding to put down roots. They do not want to move from pillar to post. They want stability and continuity for them-selves and their children. They do not want to uproot their children every few years to move to a new location. They also want to progress in their own careers. In a society that is leaning more and more towards two-income fami-lies, they want to establish themselves. They sometimes want it all. And so, where does this leave their partners? It leaves them going unaccompanied to posting after posting—trying to return home to visit with their families as often as possible.

While this arrangement might work for some, for others being posted to one end of Canada and having a family at the other end creates a financial burden as they try to travel back and forth as often as possible. This type of lifestyle creates more stress and widens the gap between the father and his family, not to mention the strain it must put on the couple. My generation's outlook was a lit-tle different than that of some in today's military world. The most important thing for us was family. Not *part* of a family but the family as a whole. It was more important to be together—where we lived was secondary to the well-being of the family unit. We quit our jobs and got another at our new location. We accepted this as our role—we were supporters first and foremost; becoming a career woman was a secondary goal. One has to wonder in this age of increased NATO tours and increased danger in those tours how this change in family dynamics is affecting our soldiers. They are not receiving the same level of support at a time when they need it the most.

I used to belong to a military spouses' e-mail group but they decided to toss me out. They didn't like my opinions on most things, needless to say. DH (darling husband) has 19 years in so far—he is away A LOT. For example, he left last September and came back just before Christmas and then left in February and is due to come back in June. Not overseas, but all over Canada. I decided to settle our family down a few years ago, bought a nice house in a small town, put my degree to good use, and allow him to come and go as the military dictates, and when he's done, he'll return home to us once again. I feel I'm preparing for his comfortable transition/retirement...into his second career (since he won't even be 40 upon retirement).

Reservists' Wives

Those who follow the reservists' route in the military lifestyle and then go on to become members of the regular force have the advantage of already being familiar with the military system. But often their families are not. When they are faced with becoming part of the regular military, which includes moving and changing of schools for their children, it can sometimes be overwhelming. Throw into that mix the possibility that many are leaving their family support network for the first time to move to an area where they know no one and dealing with being alone with their children while their partners are often gone, and it can be a time of huge readjustment.

My husband has just joined the Air Force Reserves as an apprentice Aircraft Maintenance Engineer. When he returns home to Edmonton from basic in Borden, Ontario, he will be employed full-time. In October, he'll be sent back to Ontario for seven months of technical training. Our two children and I will go with him and stay with family elsewhere in Ontario. Then he has 20 months of on-the-job training at which time he'll switch over to regular force.

This summer has been a trial to say the least, as it's been our first long time apart. The kids miss their daddy so much and I am quite lonely; I miss his touch, his smell and our intimacy. We've kept busy though, as there is much to do in and around the city in the summer, and I will go to Phil's graduation on August 23 and stay for a week. Phil will be home on September 9. I've been working out at the gym at the base, but I want to get more connected. I'd like to do basic next summer, but there is nothing else I can do within the military until I've completed basic. I feel a little out of place within the military community because he just started, we don't live on the base and he's only in reserve. Where do I fit in or do I?

Stay-at-home Husbands

Now more than ever, our female military members are being posted on tours alongside our male troops. Many are married, with families, and it's their husbands who remain behind to look after children, home and all. For many men, this is an entirely new role and they enter it with many mixed emotions: They are extremely proud of their wives and their commitment to their job and their country, but often this adjustment does not come easily.

I am a recently retired Chief Warrant Officer (CWO). I married a very beautiful lady who is a police officer and commander of a military police unit. During the last two years she has been gone for 18 months for various deployments. She is about to be deployed yet again. Even though I spent 20 years in the military, I find that I suck as a military spouse/'wife.'

Through the many e-mails this CWO and I exchanged, and reading between the lines of our communications, I got the impression that he was trying desperately to deal with his wife's many deployments. He included his wife in the distribution list of messages to me and I felt that his communication with me was another attempt at showing his wife how much he wanted his marriage to work and how hard he was trying to deal with all the emotions he was experiencing.

I told May that I am trying to find my place as her at-home-but-not-forgotten #1 fan, supporter, lover and confidant and I'm looking for guidelines on how to do that. I'm sure that when the workload for her eases (say about the time she steps out of the family car to be back home) that I'll know how she feels about sharing [with me] how this has all affected us. In the meantime, I WILL learn to stop persecuting her for doing what she has a passion for, for what she is excellent at doing and for doing what she feels she has had the calling to do for her troops, her country, herself and us.

I distinctly got the feeling that the CWO was really struggling with not coming first in his wife's life and with taking a back seat while she progressed in her career. They had no children, so his sole focus while being left behind was to deal with his emotions and be supportive of her, and yet there seemed to be an underlying genuine wish that he could be her main focus, as she was for him. This man's struggle is one that military wives often face—coming second in their husband's lives. The military comes first. We might not like it, but it's the nature of the beast so we acknowledge it and reluctantly accept it. Men seem to have a harder time doing this.

Having been a CWO, I understood her commitment but I've not had to be the spouse at home this much before. Obviously he was feeling the strain of his wife being gone so much. Added to that was his feeling of having been abandoned. *Her workload is such that she doesn't have the time to be my wife. She only has the time to be the unit's commander. So, I added a stress factor onto her that was multiplied to the nth degree. I did not realize that she was THAT busy. She has NO quiet time to tell me much at all. I went to see her about a week ago and the main conversation was that she wasn't sure that she could provide what I needed to have in our marriage. She wanted to discuss a separation. Well, I was quick to point out that we already are separated (geo-graphically). I fully understood what she meant. The separation is induced by the US Army.*

The discussion that followed was painful and one that makes you sick to your stomach. She will be leaving the country this Saturday for six months. She very much thrives on the challenge that she is given. I am laying out a plan to find the demons inside me. If she and I end our marriage, I'll still have those demons unless I address them. In the meantime, I began learning my role as a military 'wife'...I have been through two previous marriages and have yet to have children. When May left this time, she promised that we would begin a family upon her return. Since she is not sure that she wants to be married, I await to see if that will transpire. I'm not holding my breath. I am hopeful.

My heart went out to him as he struggled with being separated from his wife one more time, and his dreams of starting a family seemed to be slipping further away each time his wife took on another assignment—away from home. Having children is not something you can accomplish easily when there is physical distance between a couple and this man seemed to feel having children was just beyond his grasp. In fact, the possibility of having a committed, loving marriage also seemed to be slipping slowly through his fingers.

They both seemed to be at odds—her career obviously came first, and he wasn't comfortable with that and didn't see any possibility of that changing. However, he did try to understand, to be supportive. They had a chance to meet in Germany during her tour in Bosnia, and he had high expectations for a wonderful reunion. *When we had the chance to meet up in Germany, I dragged my feet as to making all the arrangements. I know that this spoke volumes about many things. As a man, I tend to accomplish things on an 'as needed' basis. I tend to procrastinate.* Obviously many emotions came into play as he prepared for this reunion—excitement about being together again but apprehension as to whether they would be able to settle some outstanding issues between them. He had kept things from her concerning everyday events at home so as not to distract her from her demanding job, and she felt out of sight, out of mind. They just didn't seem to be on the same wavelength and the gap between them appeared to be widening. Communication, which is pivotal in marriage, especially in a military marriage, was sadly lacking.

When we met up in Germany there was an immediate sense of distance. She admitted so herself. When she left to deploy there was so much love welling in me that I would never have thought that we would ever feel distance between us. But there it was. The trip was for nine days. It took the better part of that for a real comfort level to develop. Intimacy did follow but feeling close was a chore. Upon her return to the USA (at the end of her tour), I was overwhelmed with emotions. When she stepped off the plane I could only cry like a child that had been reunited with his mother. I [attribute] it to being reunited with my soul mate. At that moment I was able to finally stop holding back the tears. Finally I could let go all my emotions that I had stifled. At that time May said: 'I'm home now…why are you crying?' And it was difficult to explain. But she was home and that was all that mattered. NOW…we could get on with our life together.

Over the next two years, his wife was constantly called away and their continuing separations began to take their toll. He felt he was still sliding down the priority ladder as she accepted assignment after assignment—regardless of his feelings, or so it seemed to him.

We had had little chance to regain our closeness before she accepted another assignment. She accepted it with little or no hesitation. This airport was only an hour north of us. My work schedule did in fact allow me to go see her, but I also felt that she did not need her husband distracting her from a very important assignment. I also continued to persecute the military through her for doing its part in being a detriment to our life together. So there she was on orders again. Serving her country and state.

In late December she got word that another military police company was about to be placed on alert—most likely to Afghanistan. They wanted to offer her first shot at commanding this unit. It is now approximately 13 months after she started the Bosnia duty (pre-deployment duties included). She wanted to know if I was going to divorce her if she took command of this unit. I had no good answer to give. The only answer I had was to say that our marriage was already suffering. To honestly believe that her taking [this] command would have no further detriment to our relationship was absurd. I could not bless this. After much soul searching she declined the offer (which she had the option to do). But…she was, in my opinion, devastated by missing this opportunity in her life. I was devastated that she would have so little regard for our relationship and could even place it dead last.

In February of 2002, she told me that she was not sure that she wanted to be married anymore. A good deal of this had to do with my persecuting her. More of this had to deal with me not feeling good about my current job and myself. This lends itself to all kinds of bad things in a relationship. We discussed all of the 'issues' that she had bottled up inside her. At first I was quiet. I knew that it was time to listen and not talk. I tried to absorb everything. Afterward, I attempted to list what I could to rectify the current situation. No one I know can change overnight but I desired to honor how she felt and to find solutions to our problems. At first it was slow going. But I felt that she reluctantly began to see that I was sincere. So she ended her orders in mid May 2002 and we began to focus on our marriage. She was VERY reluctant at first but she did in fact begin to participate (no better description). I felt things were going much better. This continued through October 2002. We had gone on vacation with her folks. We all had a wonderful time—not a care in the world. I felt that we had really come so far back into our relationship—back to a better place. I felt that we were back on a better track.

Two days after our return from vacation, she got the call to command a unit that was slotted to go to another country. In my opinion she was going to accept—period—despite my objections. She did, in fact, agree. She went with the unit. At first things went well, but then I began to suffer what I can only [describe as] an anxiety attack. I missed her and I felt that her lack of ability to pay attention to me was a bad sign. As her workload continued to keep her from babying me, I continued to stress. This culminated in her reaching the conclusion again about not wanting to be married.

We agreed to use this time to find where our heads needed to be. We are still communicating now that they are there and have communications ability. I am taking this time to focus on what my problems are and me. The two past marriages are most likely taking a toll on me that I need to come to grips with. I also need to find out what other garbage I have in my emotional trash can that I need to empty. May and I have been married three and a half years. The distance to me is there because the damn military has not allowed us a fair chance to be married.

Sadly, communication between the CWO and me came to an end a short time later. My messages inquiring how he was doing and letting him know I was thinking of him remained unanswered. Perhaps things became too painful for him to continue sharing. He'd had his military career and retired to a second career outside the military. She obviously wanted a career more than she wanted her marriage. Had he not pressed so much for her to remain home with him would their marriage have succeeded? It's hard to say. Indications are, from what he did share with me, that she did try to cut back on her commitments to the military, to spend more time with him but wasn't happy doing so. It seemed that he was working hard to save his marriage and she was just working hard. To me, it was obvious that they wanted different things. Sometimes love just isn't enough.

Although I heard only one side of the story, his writings do show a danger in a two-career military family when one or both spouses are continually required to be away from home. The fact that they had no children was a blessing, because when children are brought into such a career-driven atmosphere, that is combined with long absences of one or both parents, the children suffer the most.

One can understand the emotions this CWO and his partner were going through while trying to deal with the demands of a challenging lifestyle. Of course, those with children face a whole different set of challenges. But many, many of the men who stay at home are meeting these challenges head-on and handling them all extremely well. One such man told me his biggest problem was assuring people he really did know how to cook and he wasn't starving, nor were his children, while his wife was on tour. In fact, he seemed really proud of himself when he told me about preparing a dinner party for eight people that was quite successful.

As I looked around his spotless home with no signs of dust, we sat in the living room sharing a cup of tea. I glanced at the numerous healthy houseplants that surrounded the living room and asked him how many he had killed since his wife left. With a slightly embarrassed tone, he informed me that there was one in the laundry room that he forgot about—but that was all.

One family physician that I spoke with told me how impressed she was with the husbands who accompanied their wives, and often their children, to appointments. Overall she found them very committed, concerned parents and husbands—and so they are. Those men who are left behind gain a much better appreciation for the role wives traditionally play, and that, in turn, makes them better partners.

Military Wives

On September 28th of this year, I will become a Royal Canadian Navy Wife! Help! I'm at a total loss now. Our wedding was supposed to be next May with 250 guests. Now it's this September with 75 guests in my grandparents' backyard. I'm assuming this will be the first of many concessions I will be making, now that I'm about to marry someone owned by the Armed Forces. I guess I'm looking for anything that is going to help me make this transition into what I know is a totally different life than I have ever had before. I'm the type of person who has to do research to know what she is in for. Any help, suggestions, resources you can suggest would be greatly appreciated.

When examining just what constitutes the military family, we quite often don't consider how civilians perceive us. As a columnist who has a regular weekly column in the *Pembroke Daily Observer* in Pembroke, Ontario, I have the unique opportunity of writing whatever comes to mind for my column, "Home Sweet Home." Once or twice a year, I write about what I know best: the military community, and in particular, military wives. Such was the case just before our troops in Petawawa started their tour in Afghanistan. I thought it was the right time to again mention the sacrifices our military families make. It was important at this particular time to acknowledge the emotions of this 'tour like no other.' But, when you are in the public eye, even for a short period of time, you leave yourself open to criticism. While I respect everyone's opinion and their right to express it, I was dismayed at the following letter to the editor that also appeared in the *Pembroke Daily Observer*. This is the mindset that I have worked so hard for so many years to change—it's obvious that I still have more work to do.

Re: 'In praise of military spouses' by Dianne Collier. I enjoy Mrs. Collier's columns very much; however I find her constant defense of the military unnecessary. I have nothing against the military. I have lost relatives on the front lines, have had others come back with unhealthy minds and have some still in the military, living the good and the bad as we all are.

Every lifestyle is challenging. However, military spouses are not the only spouses who take on dual roles during deployments. Many jobs take the breadwinner out on the road, alone, in dangerous traffic, against the elements and to strange places.

We all pay heavily for freedom. Military spouses are no different. We also do what we have to during these trying times but we don't have the shared spirit of a military family. Most of us have our own families, isolated from co-workers.

We might look forward to building equity in a home and putting down roots, but we are more likely to lose our jobs and uproot to find other work. There is nothing stopping military people from purchasing a house; I know several that do despite the knowledge their roots are short and temporary. What is wrong with that? Knowing is better than wondering.

Yes, we decorate a home if we can afford one, but it does not last a lifetime. An advantage for military spouses is moving, because a change of scenery can be refreshing. As for the room combos in PMQs [Permanent Married Quarters]—no one needs showrooms—most of us don't have them.

Military people get to see different parts of the world and form a close bond with people in similar circumstances. By moving frequently, military families also don't have time to become enemies with their neighbors and usually try to work out any problems to make their brief time together peaceful.

As for changing schools, this can be a positive experience for military children because it gives them more life experience as they see how communities and people differ. This better prepares them for life as they grow up and move out on their own.

In or out of the military, spouses are not always going to be at family functions, which is why we all need to count on each other—that's what a family is all about.

We have all lost spouses on the job or to injury. Our country asks just as much from us as it does from the military. I am proud of our military and also of our working people. We all do our part to make this country great. As one military man once said to me: 'It's all in a day's work and life's experiences.'
—Mrs. Jane Doe

In response, the following letter to the editor was also printed in the *Pembroke Daily Observer* and I eventually spoke with the writer. She was incensed at the comments of Mrs. Jane Doe and I could tell that she was still upset as we talked. She explained that she was so upset by this lady's comments that it took some time for her to compose a "reasonable" response that would be suitable for publication.

Regarding the letter to the editor suggesting that Dianne Collier may be defending the military too much. Dianne Collier wisely follows the recommendation to writers, to write what you know.

The military community is very sympathetic to the hazards and demands that many people experience in their lives and work, simply because it bumps up against that reality on a regular basis.

The military community is full of young people in their prime. Spouses and children were ignored in the past as 'excess baggage.' People such as Dianne Collier did much to give them a voice. It is now recognized that family plays a big part in the emotional support our peacekeeping troops need. The support network is growing and it's about time.

The military life comes with a large helping of loneliness. It is not an easy life. The spouse or parent is absent, with shift work or courses or special duties. Frequent moves are disrupting as school curriculums vary from province to province. Children never get to grow up with a best friend. They are often transient outsiders in their civilian community and often the victims of discrimination.

The plus side is that eventually they will have a network of friends from the military community around the world. It is not easy to explain this to a six-year-old, however, when everything in the child's world has changed and no one will be his friend.

The military teaches family to be resilient and ready for anything or it breaks them. It's hard to constantly train in warfare and come home to be Mommy, Daddy or loving spouse. It is not easy for military personnel and their spouses to be on the move and away from parents, sisters, brothers, aunts, uncles, teachers, friends you grew up with, or even the minister that married you. Their life goes on without you, and you miss out on all the little things that make relationships so valued and strong in a community. You hardly recognize the old place for changes while you were away. In the past, there were many well-thumbed copies of Doctor Spock to help decide what to do about that sick child in the middle of the night. Mom or Grandma was not easily accessible, and it is always difficult to find a new family doctor.

In the past, there was no help dealing with the stress of a spouse reliving the stink and filth and atrocities, experienced on tours and night after night in nightmares. Speaking up and speaking out is what brought improvements.

Support in the military community is building. Today, technology also allows greater access to family and friends, thank heaven. Friendships made are intense and often survive years of separations. Happy people remain basically happy in the military life. The grumpy ones carry that with them, too. Thankfully for everyone (until retirement) they move on. Your speaking out urged me to do so, too, and I thank you for that. We need to understand that the points of view of others are not too different from our own.

This next response was forwarded to the newspaper but not published; however, a copy was also sent to me via e-mail. Obviously, this lady also had strong feelings on the original letter and her response deserves equal reading.

As a military wife, I proudly wear 'my invisible uniform' with no expectations of special recognition. However, I do not appreciate someone lessening my lifestyle and role as a military wife.

Although Mrs. Jane Doe certainly is entitled to her opinion and is free to express it (a freedom given to Canadians by the blood of our soldiers), I have to strongly disagree with her attempt at simplifying the military lifestyle with easy, uninformed answers to military family issues.

Firstly, having spouses traveling on "dangerous roads" is certainly a hardship for any family. However, it cannot be compared to the family of a soldier who is fighting in Iraq or Afghanistan or anywhere else while dodging landmines and snipers and air raids. It's comparing apples and oranges.

Secondly, in most cases, the only people who really get to 'see the world' are the soldiers themselves. The families are left behind where wives deal with all aspects of the family on their shoulders alone. Mrs. Doe's answer to moving frequently saying 'a change of scenery being refreshing' is obtuse. Although that can be the case for a family who's made a unanimous decision to move to a new place, it is not at all the same as a soldier receiving an e-mail saying you WILL move to a certain place at a certain time. The spouse must now quit her job and move there most likely to become unemployed—only the soldier is guaranteed employment upon arrival. The children must leave their school and friends and find new ones. Trying to tell children that they have to leave everything familiar to them because of Dad's job is not an easy thing to do no matter how positive you try to make it seem. They are bound to be resentful and the soldier/father must deal with the fact that his children are resentful, ultimately, against him no matter how short-term it may be.

Thirdly, I agree that spouses being absent from family functions are certainly a possibility for any family. However, it is not as common in any of my civilian friends' lives. They balk at the thought of their husbands not being there for the birth of their children or for other equally important events. They cannot comprehend how that's 'normal' to me.

Lastly I'd like to address the comment 'our country asks just as much from us as it does from the military.' I have only one question: When was the last time Canada asked anything of you, Mrs. Doe?

I have discussed the original letter during several talks I have given—only to emphasize how misinformed civilians can be about our lifestyle. I feel the letter writer's mindset wouldn't change if we were to have a polite conversation on her views, but I would love to invite her to walk a mile in the shoes of any military wife and hope that this experience would give her a much different, realistic perspective on just what our life is truly like. Whenever her letter is read to a group, you can visibly see the audience reacting. They are indignant, angry and hurt—and so they should be.

I am a new military wife. When I married I stayed in Ottawa for a while as my career was very important to me. I decided last year that it was time I joined [my husband] in Petawawa. Going from Ottawa to Petawawa is a huge lifestyle change as there are no jobs in what I am qualified for....

When I married I knew what I was getting into. The lifestyle is different and by rights you as a spouse give up a lot to support what your spouse has chosen to do. I find that a lot of military wives expect to be babysat all the time; there are a lot of them that do nothing but whine and cry and expect the military to help them out with everything. I left a job and prospects to move here—my choice—and as a result, it has turned out to be the best decision.

I know life is tough with hubby away a lot on exercise and on TDs [Temporary Duty] but we as wives agreed to this. The military has changed in the last 10 to 20 years. Gone are the days of only one TD; now they are doing more than that. I find that the wives of yesterday are behind the times and really have no understanding of what it is like to be military wife today.

While I totally disagree with this lady's assumption that wives of yesterday do not understand the challenges facing today's military wives, I will admit that some of the challenges today were not challenges yesterday. However, I think our young, new wives of today need to understand the wives of yesterday because their stresses were greater and lasted longer, particularly the ladies whose husbands served in WWII and the Korean War. They didn't have e-mail, or constant connection with their partners. Many never heard from their husbands for three to five years and didn't even know if they were alive or dead. I can't begin to imagine how stressful that must have been for them.

Each generation of military wives has its own stressors and challenges. In my generation, which is the one just retiring, I didn't have to deal with the constant tours today's wives must contend with. But, at the same time, I didn't have all the support networks in place that are available today— even the connection between units and spouses has improved by leaps and bounds. We never heard of a briefing for the wives. We didn't have Military Family Resource Centres or all the employment advantages available today, such as free resume preparation, job transfer, and financial allowances for this and that. And yet, my generation had it so much better than those who came before us. I suggest that today's wives need to mix and mingle with those from past generations to get a better appreciation for all they have.

The bottom line for all of us wives, past, present and in the future, is that we want our partners home with us, safe and happy, and sometimes we have to settle for just a little of each. It's the nature of the beast we call military life.

We have 'chosen' our paths as military spouses BUT that does not mean we have no right to be lonesome, afraid, worried, angry or any other emotion. Accepting our 'choice' means only that we will hang in there no matter what. If we believe for one moment that when we fell in love with our soldier we gave up the right to be human, then we will end up broken and bitter one day. That would not be a healthy lifestyle nor very supportive. Embrace your emotions, every one of them from pain and anguish to joy and pride. They will make you strong and keep you focused on the soldier you love!

So, who are we really? How do you describe a military wife? Adapt, improvise and overcome are words that so adequately describe us—they're what we do. In *Home Fires*, Jacqueline Marcipont, a military wife, explains it best. Even though her comments were written with military wives in mind, they apply equally well to girlfriends and husbands—to all who keep the home fires burning.

Home Fires

By Jacqueline Marcipont

We are those that keep the home fires burning. We leave our previous lives behind us, to join with someone who is often gone. We support them, and encourage them to succeed in their chosen field of work.

We are always ready to pack up and move at a moment's notice. With no hesitation, we leave behind our home, our friends, our jobs; and follow.

We strive to be understanding and supportive. We listen wordlessly to the horrors that they have seen, and pray silently that they will not be hurt.

We try to comprehend the changes that we see in them each time that they return. We accept them, and learn to love them all over again for who they are.

We take our children to lessons and sporting events alone, taking hundreds of pictures to put in albums; so not as much of their childhood is missed.

We tuck them in at night and explain why only one parent is there to say 'goodnight.' We reassure them constantly that even though they're absent, their other parent loves them very, very much.

We go to bed alone at night, and cry for the partner that is sorely missed. We wake up to a new day ready to go on—and keep the Home Fires Burning.

Chapter 2

Support Systems

*Supporting these troops is not something that I think
about doing, it is something I do every day without thinking.*

There are many support systems in place within the military community, but the biggest support must come from spouses for their partners. That is our role—to support—just as any spouse would do regardless of their partner's occupation. Many times the support the spouses provide can come with a whole kit-bag-full of emotions. But the bottom line is that we recognize the dangerous job our serving partners do and we must make every effort not to add to their stress level.

One military spouse expressed just that so well:

My husband has been in the military for 11 years now and we have been married for eight years. I knew what his job was when I married him. I knew that UN [United Nations] tours were a reality and would happen. They did. Yes, it was difficult—especially with two small children under the age of two. I know it is even harder when you are posted away from family and friends. And no, the military way of life in general is not easy. Low pay, poor housing, lack of support from communities, blah blah blah. But the one place we should be able to count on for support—NOT CRITICISM—is other military wives and personnel. The spouses who constantly complain, whine, and carry on about how rotten the military way of life is should basically put up or shut up.

Our men need our support and we can still be women of the '90s by [showing it.] Our men count on us, family, co-workers and the community for as much support as they can get. I am very proud of my husband, my friends' husbands, and the job that they do. My children miss their father when he is away—not just on tours but on exercises as well—and I try to explain to them a little about the importance of Daddy's job and how he keeps us safe. This is my duty to the military—to be supportive as well as understanding of the way of life we have and have CHOSEN. No it is not easy, and it is not for every woman, but you have to have courage and trust and love to continue in this lifestyle.

Please support our troops wherever they may be serving. Pray for those who do not have the same advantages as us, and be proud that your spouse is part of the Canadian Military. I know I am, and all I can do is keep my chin up and deal with one day at a time and be grateful for my friends and the country I live in. I'M PROUD TO BE A MILITARY SPOUSE.

I truly believe in what my husband has been trained to do. The troops that we send on these missions do us all proud. Supporting these troops is not something that I think about doing, it is something I do every day without thinking. My family has a long record of service to our country and we should all be proud that even with cutbacks they still do a wonderful job.

Quality of Life

The catchphrase in the military community these days is certainly 'Quality of Life' and that, above all else, is what the majority of spouses wanted me to cover in this book. But, as many have said, quality of life is really a catch-all because it means different things to different people. What would improve the quality of life for one family might not be high on the priority list for another.

The question raised is how far should the Quality of Life (QOL) Directorate go in providing support to not only our military members, but to their families as well. Where should the line be drawn? The answers to these questions were wide-ranging.

To find out just what this directorate was all about, I traveled to its headquarters in Ottawa and met with a wonderfully compassionate, caring lady, Commander Heather Armstrong, the Family Policy Team Leader for the QOL. I was immediately struck by her knowledge of military family issues and by her obvious commitment to her new position. A member of the QOL team for only five months when we met, Commander Armstrong's strong sense of where we are and where we need to go was impressive. Since her husband, also a member of the Canadian Forces, was away on a six-month tour, she was living the emotional roller coaster all spouses experience when being separated from their partner for a long period of time. That fact alone certainly added to her being the right person for the job.

It's amazing how preconceived notions can be so wrong. I went to this meeting fully expecting to find a few staff members crowded into an overused work area so typical of many military offices. Instead I found a brand new building with workspaces for approximately 20 staff, spread out in a maze of cubicles. My first impression—that this is a well-organized group—was followed by a sense that DND (Department of National Defence) was indeed serious in it's commitment to providing a better quality of life for all, and that they were providing the proper tools for the QOL staff to shape this directorate into a positive, supportive group who will certainly make a difference in the military community. My previous impression that QOL issues were being addressed only as a secondary priority and by very few people couldn't be farther from the truth and that certainly was a pleasant surprise. The Directorate itself stood up on September 1, 2001, and within one year not only had the staff increased from seven to 20, but 68 of the 89 Standing Committee on National Defence and Veterans Affairs (SCONDVA) recommendations had been implemented.

The fact that most respondents to my questionnaire knew next to nothing about the QOL team appears to be symptomatic of a certain level of mistrust of the system, since fear of the unknown is always difficult to deal with. When asking spouses if the QOL team adequately notifies them of its efforts on the families' behalf, most spouses shouted "No!" Almost as many said they were not aware of the QOL Directorate's mandate.

All of that being said, I hope this chapter will provide many assurances that although new to the military community, the QOL office is working hard to become a cohesive, important part of our lifestyle. They recognize areas that need improvement and are working on making positive changes. But, as we all know, change takes time, it doesn't happen overnight—especially in the maze of DND.

One of the areas that appears to need work is the disseminating of information about what the QOL Directorate has accomplished since its inception.

Military families need to be kept in the know. Just posting information on a website isn't adequate—many families do not have access to the Internet. And yet, finding a way to reach our military families can be a full-time job in itself. Families tend to view new programs as being part of "the system." If the QOL Directorate is responsible for offering a particular benefit, then families should know about that. Otherwise, the credibility and success of the QOL Directorate will take a much longer time in coming.

When finalizing this book, a year after I first met Commander Armstrong, I contacted her to see what had changed in the past year. I was very pleased to see that although some of her military staff had changed, Commander Armstrong's position as Family Policy Team Leader is now a civilian position, which means that she is now filling the position as a civilian and will be able to provide continuity, something that is vital to ensure the smooth flow of the entire section.

Currently, the QOL website (http://www.dnd.ca/hr/qol/engraph/home_e.asp) is being updated as is the Military Family National Advisory Board (MFNAB) website (http://www.mfnab.forces.gc.ca/engraph/home_e.asp). It is hoped that more than the basic information will be provided on these websites when the changes have been completed. Military families need to know more than they do, and for those that have access to the Internet, it's certainly the place to start looking.

I think we need to talk about the 'Quality of Life' that the military likes to preach about instead of the pay raises. The military likes to talk about quality of life just to keep the media off their scent. When was the last time any of us got a military flight? I am posted clean across Canada away from my family and quality of life makes it impossible for me to go and at least visit them. Something needs to be done regarding this quality of life situation. Ha. Ha. What a joke!

The following entry appeared in a military wives' e-mail forum and is a typical example of the way the Internet is used today by military spouses to gather information before making a decision. However, the danger in asking for advice is that you might not always receive the proper advice—something I have noticed from time to time. Well-meaning ladies are free to give their opinion—but some of their "advice" has me shuddering when I read it because it is based on assumptions and half-truths and many times garnered just from casual conversations with their partners. While the following exchange might not fit into the "untrue" category, I caution everyone to ensure that if you are seeking answers, you direct your questions to the right place.

There is a new mandate out. Quality of Life Postings instead of compassionate postings. They say that they do not affect the career of the member. On the DND website it says the same. We are looking at [a compassionate posting] to get closer to an ill family member, but I wanted to know what other people have heard about this type of posting or [if they have] experienced it themselves. I would love to hear your input.

I doubt the quality of life postings are very different from compassionate ones. They may say in the books that it doesn't affect your career, but what is on the books and what actually happens are very different. Your reason for wanting one sounds very understandable; however, there is always the risk that people will use them just to get out of sailing, like so many people do with stress, compassionate and medical leave. That is part of the reason so often it is the same people sailing all the time and others stay ashore and never sail, and I fear that 'quality of life postings' would just make this problem worse. I myself know too many people who when it comes to actually doing time sailing, run to the hospital or the padre, whatever. This is unfair to those that end up going from ship to ship to cover those who just don't want to sail. If there are such things as quality of life postings, I hope they are used sparingly and responsibly. Just my thoughts...

The following comments were submitted in answer to the question *Where is the Quality of Life we women deserve?* that was posted on the discussion page of my website. This military wife's comments and responses to her statements from other wives provide a wide variety of opinions. Only you can decide where you sit on this sharp, pointed, picket fence.

Where is the Quality of Life we women deserve? I have been in the military world since my childhood and then I married into it. Here is my story about a typical marriage to a military man and why so many women wind up divorcing their husbands.

Without hesitation I have followed my husband to his posting choices. I have left good jobs and comfortable homes. Often as soon as I became familiarized with my surroundings, it was time to pack up and leave again. Easy to accomplish when you are young and you have no children. Now that my daughters (11 years and 6 years) are growing up and are both in school, my perception has changed.

I want my daughters to live where they will keep up with their mother tongue and get to know our relatives. As we are a Francophone family, being away from our families has become tremendously difficult. My youngest has seen her grandparents three times in six years. It is not fair to her or them. They need to get to know each other better. Which brings me to the problems of getting a babysitter or wanting to get away for the weekend, as social workers often suggest getting a babysitter to [be able to have some time away from the house to] help rediscover each other. Unfortunately, we cannot experience that pleasure, as it is too expensive to hire a sitter for a whole weekend. That is why I believe that it is important to get the support and help from your family (especially when there is no cost associated with it).

I'm sure that I'm not the only one when I say I'm fed up in spending thousands of dollars in plane tickets to go visit family. I would like for once to be able to spend that amount on worthwhile trips like Disney World or save the money to buy a home. Not that visiting our family isn't worthwhile, but if I was closer or at least in driving distance, I wouldn't have to save up all that money to go visit them. Not everyone can afford to travel every year to see his or her relatives. I know I can't. When you spend special holidays like Christmas without Grandpa, Grandma, aunts, uncles, sisters, brothers and cousins, your friends become your family and you feel left out of your real family activities. It becomes discouraging and frustrating.

The worst is when your spouse is away on TD [temporary duty], courses, or serving in a UN/NATO tour where we are left alone to handle everyday tasks. I have been raising our two daughters basically on my own (a full-time job I might add), keeping the house up, cleaning, cooking, mowing the lawn, shoveling on cold winter days, bringing kids back and forth from extracurricular activities, school meetings, working a full-time job, which I must keep to survive in this world. Let's not forget the added stress when the car breaks down, which seems to happen only when hubby is away, or an electrical appliance needs repair or a toilet is plugged. Whatever the circumstances, it is hard to handle when you don't have your family's support.

Which brings me to one of my pet peeves, taking up on offers for help from friends. I'm sure we've all experienced asking for help only to hear an excuse for [a friend] to say no. It has happened to me so often. It is not easy for a woman to ask another woman's husband for help. As you know, people talk and start rumors and things get out of hand, and then you look like the villain when all you did was to take them up on their offers to help. There are always the worries of not being able to handle it and looking like a failure to your peers, feeling left out, not clued in on the changes, like the world continued without you, not having time to read the newspaper, let alone sit down and relax. Relax: there's something that I'm often told to do but somehow never get around to. It's certainly not in my vocabulary these days.

Over the past 13 years, I have spent nights alone while my husband spent his serving his country. I waited patiently for his return from a six-month tour to Cyprus, followed him to Germany for 4.5 years, most of which was spent on exercises and away from home (nine months out of 12). Then we moved to Ottawa for two years, the only time that I was close to my family. I've been to Cold Lake for six years (which included a UN tour to Bosnia), Innuvik and, since July 2000, a posting to BC (sailing on the HMCS Ottawa *in Esquimalt), and of course the numerous TDs.*

I am long overdue for a well-deserved break from this life. I miss the warmth and hugs that one should get when feeling down and hurt even if it's because of a small problem. I miss the support you get without being judged or advice given without pushing, letting you know that they will always be there even if it's only to help you gain your confidence.

I especially miss my twin sister that I have been apart from for over 11 years. She respects who I have become and encourages me through changes. We talk on the phone for hours, communicating the deepest hurts with a single word, but it is not enough. I'm exhausted and feel I can no longer continue without the support of my family. My friends think of me as a very strong, independent individual and even though they say nothing, I know they slowly see me sinking into depression.

We have tried to move the girls and myself to Borden, where my twin resides, through a Quality of Life and a Compassionate posting. Both requests were refused with the explanation that we do not fit the criteria. My husband has been in the military for 16 years; he has always given one hundred percent. His career manager felt that I was being too difficult in refusing to move to Esquimalt. This would have meant being further away from my family. My husband would be gone at sea most of the time, I would be totally alone in a new environment, and it would be even more awkward to ask for help if needed. Furthermore, having the financial burden of living in an outrageously expensive city would not help. That is why I opted to stay in Cold Lake, during his sailing time, where I was comfortable and so were my daughters.

Someone once said that your life is like a car. You need to get in and drive it if you want it to get somewhere. I am doing just that, taking the driver's seat. The military has destroyed my marriage but I won't let it ruin my life. I'm tired of being alone and having to do it all. I am trying through my work, Public Service Alliance of Canada, to get deployed down East. It's not as easy as expected. This will mean that I will have to pay for my move.

Even if my husband wanted to take his release, his career manager told him that he would hold him back for six months. I do not wish for him to lose his pension or any of his benefits. In order to try to mend things between us, he will have to wait until I have secured employment in one of the eastern provinces, preferably Ontario, and then he will retire. The military life has finally taken its toll on my family. I have overcome many obstacles in the past but feel I can no longer fight this battle. All I want is to be close to my family.

It is unfortunate that the Quality of Life committee never thought of the spouses when implementing a solution to a problem. It is only meant for the military member at work. Why can't they consider a marital discord as one of the criteria?

Why are you blaming the military for all your difficulties? I agree that the Quality of Life still has room for improvement, but come on! Sounds like there might be some other issues as well here. I miss my husband when he is away, but I knew when we got together he would be away a lot. Maybe your husband should have let you know what you were getting into. Maybe if more people did that, there would be less misunderstanding about this way of life. It definitely isn't for everyone.

I understand totally a lot of what the wives are saying. However, as I married my husband before he joined, no one can say to me 'You knew what you were marrying.' So I choose to follow and go where we are sent. I agree that those close to finishing their 20 years should get considera-tion and I agree that compassionate postings should be scrutinized very care-fully. However, I also ask, didn't you agree to this lifestyle when you married your spouse? It's not the greatest and not for everyone, but I would be over-joyed to have my husband well enough to go away on exercise or on tours. You see he now has PTSD [Post Traumatic Stress Disorder] and I would gladly have him physically away and yet present in my mind rather than physi-cally here and not here emotionally. Be careful what you ask for and be thank-ful for what you have.

Thank you for the courage to speak out on the painful subject of marital breakups due to the increasing time the husbands must be away from home. Being away from family is difficult and without the flights of the service air, the cost of going to visit is out of reach for most families.

Quality of Life issues seem to be a 'smoke and mirrors' campaign for the politicians to look good to the public. How unfortunate they are not following through on the many positive proposals that have been suggested.

Living alone has become second nature to me. How sad that my husband is a stranger in his own home. He has worked too hard for his pension and would not be able to find work in his field in the civilian world.

I knew when I married [my husband] that being apart was to be expected but I had not counted on the exercises, work-up training, mock exercises in addition to the lengthy tours. In one year he was home only 50 non-consecutive days.

You both have hit the nail on the head! The frustration sometimes seems too much to take. We are going through the same things here (just fewer years of it). I chose to marry him, not the army. Although they say you marry the army first! Quality of Life seems to have no bearing on any-thing they do. My husband is part of the vanguard preparing to deploy to Afghanistan and it is so frustrating. There is absolutely no information being passed down by the unit and the media is all over the politicians' words. We have been on 48-hour notice for what seems like an eternity. I keep wondering how long they will fence-sit, how long will he be here? When will we be able to conduct a semi-normal life? Will we know first or will the politicians tell the world on the evening news again before [the notice] snakes its way down the chain of command? They talk of how vital we are to our spouses' success and how the success of a mission requires our support. When will they realize that we are human beings and we need the interaction with our spouses and families to thrive? HOHOHO Merry Christmas—will he be by my side?

I just discovered this site and finished reading your letter. I, too, am a military wife of 13 years. I can relate to most of your frustrations. We are living in Nova Scotia, have been since 1991. All of our families are in Manitoba or out west. I have been home four times since 1991, twice for a visit, and twice for funerals of my grandparents. We would like to be home to visit more, or have our extended families visit us, but as you well know us military folk aren't rich!!!

I guess my story is long, so I won't go into much detail. The main reason I was searching this site was to seek some kind of support for myself as my husband is leaving in two days for 10 months. He is going to Borden, Ontario, on a restricted posting on an occupational transfer. Yeah, believe it!

We have four kids, aged 10 to 17.5 years, and I work full-time. So, needless to say, it is going to be hard. I was hoping to e-mail women who are in this situation or who have been there, for support. This life isn't easy...and it's not for everyone. It takes a special woman to be a military wife.

I totally agree and support you and what you had to say. Just recently I was diagnosed with depression and am currently taking medication for this. I am residing on the east coast but my family is west coast. When trying for a quality of life posting, I was told that my timing was off for that. I then asked for a compassionate posting. I happened to see the letter that the social worker wrote to my doctor and there is no possible way that I would have gotten the posting.

I cannot believe how little the military cares about the dependants. They brought in this Quality of Life stuff simply to quiet the media—there is no quality of life for the dependants. Can you imagine just three days into being diagnosed with depression, a Captain military social worker telling you that your timing was all off! Needless to say, I share in your frustration and hope that your situation improves for you, as mine will not.

My husband is now leaving for six months to join the war against terrorism and not only am I not around my family when I really need them, I cannot even get a military flight as they no longer exist. I cannot afford to fly home on my own dime as I chose not to work. Yours truly in frustration.

Military Family National Advisory Board

According to the Military Family National Advisory Board's website, the MFNAB is an advisory board to the Assistant Deputy Minister Human Resources Military [ADM(HR-Mil)] and is responsible for:

advising on policy and future trends that affect military families;

advocating on behalf of military families to ensure an acceptable quality of family life for the family and the military member;

monitoring the implementation and effectiveness of the programs affecting military families; and

promoting the military family as a valuable asset to the effectiveness and operational readiness of the Canadian Forces.

Ask most military spouses if they know what this board (MFNAB) is, what its mandate is, or whether they know who their local representative is, and most will say they've never heard of them. And yet, as of May 2003, this board has had 14 meetings! Why the big secrecy? If this board is looking after the best interests of military families and there are regional representatives of military families on the board, then why don't we know who they are and what they do?

As I scanned the list of board members (24) shown on the minutes of the April 8, 2003 meeting, there were six spousal representatives. In my question-naire to the spouses, I asked them if they wanted to know more about this group and the majority said "yes." But one has to ask how can this be accom-plished. If this group oversees all policies concerning our military families, then why are they so secretive? If the military spouses on this board are repre-senting our best interests, how do they know what those best interests are if they don't consult us? One response I received to this question was that the spousal representatives keep in close contact with the MFRCs. However, since only around 10 percent of military families utilize the MFRCs, then these rep-resentatives are certainly not getting a feel for what is important to the other

90 percent of military families. There is something wrong with this picture. The MFNAB needs to make itself available to military families, to hear our concerns. Yes, this could put them on overload—particularly in light of all the issues families are concerned about today—but isn't that what they are there for, to represent ALL of us?

The MFNAB has been in existence for approximately six years and, like any new group, it took time to settle into its role, once that had been defined. That this is a very important group to military families is obvious, but does it give us another example of the system telling us what we need rather than asking us? One board member feels her work on the board is by far the most important thing that she has done. Another stated that the military spouses on the board are finally being accepted and being asked for their opinion. After six years, I would hope so.

Too many times the military operates on a "need to know" basis—and sometimes that is necessary. Families are still a low priority, but we've never expected to come first, nor should we. However, there is something fundamentally wrong with a group's claim to be looking out for our best interests when no one seems to know who that group is or what that group is doing. Again, posting information on a website is not enough. Recently, the MFNAB website went for over six months without being updated.

Both the QOL Family Team Policy section and the MFNAB have to provide more than just the basic information on their website. Military families want to know more than that—they deserve that much. Too much secrecy only increases the distrust of the system. The military family needs to be kept informed. And while I appreciate what a time-consuming job this could be, it would be time well spent if it removes some of the anxieties and misconceptions our families are now dealing with.

Peer Support

There is nothing like talking to another military wife because she is the only one who truly understands what you go through. "Been there, done that" is such a well-known saying—it's right up there with "hurry up and wait"! For the young wife just starting out, this challenging lifestyle can all seem so overwhelming. These are the ladies who need to reach out and ask for support, and it should be the seasoned military spouses' responsibility to take these "new-bies" under their wing, to offer a shoulder to cry on, a place to vent, a shared cup of tea, and the bond of friendship.

My need for peer support this time around is so truly tremendous. I'm not good at asking for help and I've trudged through the last seven years with silence and loneliness. I can't tell you how much joy and comfort you have all brought me. It's good not to feel so alone.

One military wife took the first step by sending me the following e-mail message. Sometimes putting your thoughts into words brings comfort:

Well, I am new to the military wives' club, I guess you could say, and it is really hard. I never, in all my life, could have imagined the pain in my heart every time [my husband] walked out that door for an exercise or wherever they were sending him next. I am now just getting myself ready for him to go overseas and I am trying to be strong but I really am hurting inside. I look up to the women that have been doing this for a long time. It is really hard but I love him and I wouldn't change that for the world!

It's a demanding lifestyle, there's no doubt about that. I've only been a military spouse for 10 years (not quite a seasoned veteran) but I feel that the lifestyle will either make or break a spouse. Some individuals are better at coping than others. There is no shame in saying that this isn't for you. We all have our breaking point where we just can't deal with the demands of a military spouse any more. Even with the stress of moves, deployments, etc. I can honestly say that I've traveled more and experienced things I probably never would have otherwise. Will I always feel this way? I don't know. What I do know is that my spouse is my best friend, strongest ally and supporter. It really takes a strong united couple to make the 'military way of life' work. There are lots of things I intensely dislike about DND, things I can't change. I'm sure we can all think of a few. Instead of dwelling on the bad things, I find one has to make a real effort to go ahead with their lives in spite of the demands of the military. Try to be as normal as possible.

My husband just returned from his first six-month tour in Sarajevo. The departure, the distance and the returning are not easy on either of us. I had an Air Force Dad, my first husband was an NCM [non commissioned member] first in the infantry and then as a weapons technician, and my second husband is an engineer. I have been in the Reserves for almost 12 years and work full-time in uniform. With this as a background you would think I would be prepared, yet what got me through it all was the best girlfriend in the world who was going through it at the same time (her husband being away for 13 months) and the never-ending understanding of my husband.

I moved from Ontario to Edmonton to be with my boyfriend. I left my family and friends to be with the love of my life—what an eye opener. It has been a hard adjustment for me getting used to this way of life. Jacob and I got married in 2001 and moved to Lancaster Park. I feel very alone when he goes away, be it for four days or three weeks. I try and do volunteer work at the MFRC when I am able to, but I have a severe case of depression, which affects my moods a lot, and I take medication for it. I have made some friends here and that is very helpful when my husband is away, but still I feel isolated and alone. My family and friends back in Ontario have no idea and do not understand the role of a military wife. I hope to hear from you, with any comments or advice you can pass this way, or just to make a new e-mail friend, and who knows, maybe one day we'll be posted to Petawawa.

Our lads have started to go in big numbers to the Middle East. I said my goodbye to a close friend of my husband's today. He stood at our door in his desert combats, not really wanting to go. He met his girlfriend through me and now I have got to support her through her first separation from him. She cried for half an hour on the phone last night (she is 200 miles from me). She lives away from all her family due to her job. I have told her that she has to set herself targets and projects to do while he is gone. That is the only way I have ever coped.

The Angel Book

In the spring of 2002, I met a very special military wife. She was a crafter like

I was, and although she was young enough to be my daughter, we became friends. We were involved in a volunteer project and spent time at each other's homes. When our yearly fundraiser for the Canadian Cancer Society was approaching, I organized a group of volunteers to enter a team. The fundraiser is an all-night team relay. A member from each team must continually walk or run around a track for about 12 hours. Each team member obtains sponsors who donate money to the Cancer Society. It is a friendly event in which each team tries to outdo the others in collecting the largest number of pledges.

Patti was very eager to participate in this event, as she was a cancer survivor. While she shared her story with me over a cup of tea, I marveled at how well she had handled this devastating battle and how excited and grateful she was to have overcome this tremendous challenge. She was a good person with a strong belief in God and an extremely strong sense of family.

A tradition within the relay is to have all the cancer survivors participating in the event take a victory lap around the track to start the evening's event. Knowing of Patti's deep emotional attachment to this fundraiser, I presented her with a long-stemmed rose on behalf of the team as she prepared to start her victory lap. This event is a tremendously successful one that raises large sums of money and it is also one of the biggest volunteer efforts in our community. Held on the base at CFB Petawawa, it always brings the civilian and military communities together. It's an evening of comradeship, laughter and banter, and is an absolutely wonderful event in which to take part. Everyone on our team had a wonderful time.

Just before Christmas 2002, an out-of-town member of the e-mail group I had created for military wives was to visit our area, and I had arranged for all the local girls in the group to gather at my home so we could meet her. Patti had suggested we create a craft together—an excellent idea to break the ice. Patti provided the supplies so that each lady could create an angel by the end of the afternoon. Everyone had a great time and it was wonderful for us to have a better chance to get to know each other than communicating by e-mail would allow for.

Unbeknownst to me, shortly afterwards Patti developed some health problems and by the spring of 2003 she was again on the roller coaster of visiting specialists and being told one day her cancer had returned and the next, that it had not. When I visited her at her home around this time, I was shocked to see sheer terror on her face and I knew that things weren't going well. Shortly afterwards, she was hospitalized. The last time I visited her during her hospital stay was the day she was preparing to come home. She was so excited and couldn't wait to get home to her husband and two young sons.

About a week later I thought I'd give her a call, assuming she would be well settled in at home now and might like some company (at this point her condition hadn't been confirmed). Before I could contact her, however, I ended up in the hospital myself. When I was moved out of intensive care five days later, I was put in a hospital room with one other occupant—Patti. We were both shocked to see each other, but happy to be sharing a room. It was during this time that I learned her cancer had indeed not only returned, but had spread.

When I look back several months later, I appreciate even more the quiet time that Patti and I shared in that hospital room. It was short-lived, but I experienced something in that room that I must share with all of you. It's a wonderful story of how a group of military wives banded together to offer laughter and comfort to their dying friend.

Patti had a love for angels—anyone who visited her home would see angels wherever they turned. And so these wonderful friends of Patti's borrowed some angel costumes from the military chapel and, along with one husband who acted as the photographer, they set out for Home Fires Park [a park dedicated to military spouses at CFB (Canadian Forces Base) Petawawa—the first of its kind in Canada]. Their intent was to create some funny photos. They wanted to make Patti laugh.

That first morning as Patti and I finished our breakfast, one of her friends arrived with the Angel Book. It contained all the photos that had been taken by these mischievous friends. As I lay there in the bed, I smiled as Patti laughed over and over and I heard the joy in her voice as she turned page after page of photos. The seven angels had accomplished what they set out to do—they made Patti laugh.

Afterwards, as I viewed these photos, it was obvious that these ladies thoroughly enjoyed what they did. Picture after picture showed the angels hugging a tree, holding hands in a circle representing the endless circle of true friendship, and so on. Each photo was a wonderful tribute to the lady they were created for. My first thought was to suggest that they would make a beautiful calendar. But, visitors soon arrived and there was no time for more conversation as later on that afternoon Patti was moved to another floor to receive more specialized care.

My hospital stay ended a short time later and I tried to visit with Patti at least once a week. She was such a loving, giving person that it was no surprise that friends constantly surrounded her. She welcomed as many visitors as would come—looking back I can certainly understand her not wanting to be alone—so it was impossible to have one-on-one time with her, but I will always treasure the time we had shared together in our hospital room.

About two weeks later, I did find her alone for a few minutes and the idea of the calendar was still on my mind. But what is a calendar for? It's to plan ahead, to record upcoming events. I thought that this might not be the right thing to suggest to Patti, as thinking ahead might be just too stressful for her and her friends and family. However, knowing her as I did, my heart told me to broach the subject with her. She thought it was a wonderful idea. And, since I had the equipment at home to produce the calendar, I offered to create one for her and for her seven angels. This would be my gift to her.

The point of the calendar was to allow Patti to leave a lasting gift with those special ladies who went out of their way to show her how much they loved her. And so I included an extra page in the calendar so that Patti could write a special message to each one of her friends.

As I was assembling the calendar, I decided I needed to include a picture of Patti since I was naming the calendar Patti's Angel Calendar. I remembered the day at my kitchen table making angels with Patti and the girls, and realized that a group picture had been taken that day. I thought it would be perfect for this project. As I scanned the picture and set out to crop Patti's image from the group, I suddenly realized that to her left in the picture was part of a small Christmas tree that was hanging on my wall. All I ever put on it are crocheted angels made by yet another military wife, my son's mother-in-law. Somehow those angels needed to stay with Patti's image—and they did.

When the project was finished I was just delighted with people's response to it. Patti was so pleased and it gave me pleasure to see her happy to be able to give something back to these ladies who had supported her and were her friends. I offered to make calendars for Patti's family, and over the next several weeks, I found myself busy printing and assembling more and more calendars. Once the count reached 35, I stopped keeping track. But finally I had managed to give Patti all that she wanted.

I printed up one last calendar (for myself) and headed to the hospital. When I arrived I was shocked at the change in Patti's condition since I had seen her last. She was unable to sign my calendar and passed away less than two days later. Patti Dawe was only 35 years old. I draw comfort from knowing that I added some joy to her last days and the note I received in the mail shortly before her death that read "…I am so glad you are my friend. Love Patti" is one of my treasured possessions.

Military Family Resource Centres (MFRCs)

Our MFRCs have been in existence for over 12 years and offer a wide variety of services to support military families. According to the Director Military Family Support website, the Military Family Support Program (MFSP) is implemented through Canadian Military Family Resource Centres at all Canadian bases, wings and stations, as well as some foreign locations. Professional staff and volunteer provide services in five mandated areas: information and referral; children and youth; education and quality of life, which includes deployment assistance and employment assistance; volunteer development and involvement; and prevention/intervention. While each MFRC can't be everything to everyone, their importance in the military community is undeniable.

In my research I was surprised to find that only a very small percentage of military families utilize the resources the MFRCs offer (10 percent is the figure being bandied around by many). Many dual-income families state that between the demands of full-time jobs and family responsibilities there is not enough free time left to access the MFRC. This all-too-common situation, coupled with so many of our families now living off-base and often a fair distance from the MFRC locations, does not make it convenient for families to make use of the MFRCs.

However, for the approximately 10 percent who do utilize the MFRCs, they are a lifesaver. Moving to a new location where you don't know anyone can be very intimidating, but our families draw comfort from the fact that on each base they move to there will be an MFRC there to welcome them. A place to start making new friends. A place where everyone understands the emotions of this nomadic lifestyle.

 I want to say that the MFRC in Greenwood is very responsive to the spouses' needs when the men are deployed. We receive regular

newsletters and warm-line calls as frequently or infrequently as the spouse wants; also there is a small core of us spouses who have 'Payday Dinners' with daycare provided free at the MFRC if requested. The only problems I have are not with the MFRC. My son's swim club is from 4 to 5 and I get home from work at 5. Interestingly, the MFRC offered to pick him up and take him over on those days I have trouble leaving work in time to get him there. They are also very quick to offer help when I have teen problems (I have three teens—all girls!) I can honestly say I dread the thought of leaving this base because this is the best treatment I have ever received.

I too am from Greenwood and I find the MFRC to be very disappointing. If you have an under-four-year-old child, there is not much to do with them there. I have a house full of toys so why would I want to take my child (who is only 20 months old) there to play with the same toys as he has at home? He is too young to really interact with other children.

I also think the classes that are offered are for such a short period of time for such a ridiculous amount of money. I don't participate in the clubs like ceramics and such because most of the members are really cliquey and don't come off as warm and friendly. Not to mention the people they do let in have such bad reputations for being gossipy backstabbers that I would be embarrassed for someone to see me with them. So I guess you could say since my DH has not had any deployments, I have no need or interest in the MFRC. That's all I need is for the whole base to know about my business. I just wish they centered more things on young toddlers.

I have one complaint about the resource center on the base where we are posted. I just happen to live in another town outside the base. I felt that I was alienated when I phoned for a service. I happen not to live in PMQs but elected to own a house instead. When I phoned I asked about babysitters and they said they only had the service for the PMQ areas or the immediately surrounding area. Then I asked if they knew of a service in the town that I live in and they didn't have any information available. Didn't even say that they would look into it and find information for me. You know, I am a military wife and I should be able to have the same services if I live on-base or not. Since then I do not get involved with the resource center.

The Edmonton Garrison MFRC is excellent. The staff members there are great and are always ready to help with an answer to a question or provide an ear to listen. A lot of activities are geared towards spouses with children. I don't have children, but get involved by volunteering at family day or helping with childcare for women whose husbands are deployed. This keeps me busy and involved while my spouse is deployed.

One of the biggest hurdles I have experienced as a full-time working spouse and mother living in civilian housing is that most of the activities are geared around stay-at-home moms. All the fun activities, play groups, etc., are all during the weekday.

On occasion I have taken a day off to participate in Base activities, or sent our daycare provider (who was not made to feel very welcome since she was an 'outsider'). Even swimming lessons for my two toddlers are from 4 to 7 p.m., which is next to impossible to participate in when I only finish work at 5 p.m.

As for families of deployed members, I am told that we don't have evening activities because of lack of participation, which is really sad (probably because this is a small base). It would also be nice to have free daycare provided when adult activities are going on. The North Bay MFRC does do a great job with their newsletter and it is definitely something I look forward to receiving. And I have just received my first 'warm line' call, which was also comforting.

If the units offered as much cooperation as the MFRC does in Edmonton especially regarding support for the families when husbands are away on a mission; if the units were more attentive to the needs of the families. IF...—our world would be almost perfect!

I went to the MFRC in Petawawa for a meeting and two staff members were talking about a military wife who had been there that morning crying over financial matters. Her husband wasn't sending money to her. They were discussing her problems where others, including myself, could hear. The confidentiality at the MFRC is not as it should be. I know I would never go there if I had any problems—I'd go to my friends first.

To me, the MFRC is more a place to get out of your own four walls. There isn't enough for people who don't have children. The drop-in center should have more activities for these people to draw them out of their homes.

This tour is harder than before. The military is not like it used to be years ago—it was more family-oriented then. My husband has been in for 21 years and I felt more welcome then. Sometimes you feel like you are hung out to dry and you either sink or swim.

Pizza Party for kids at the Toronto MFRC: There was one other family there with three kids. I was told not to bring my little one because it was only for three-year-olds and up. Mind you, the lady running it brought her own child with her who was under three. The other family there was asking me how I found out about the pizza party so I let [the woman] know that I had called (the MFRC).

We both discussed with the deployment coordinator what the procedure was with reference to information from the Toronto MFRC when a spouse deploys. She told me (honest) that it was my own fault [that I didn't know] because my husband should have come in to see them before he left. She said it is part of the out clearance (it's not, probably should be though). She wasn't rude in her manner, just not very helpful. I know I sound like I am just bitching, but I'll tell you it was fun for the kids to play around at the center, but that was about it. She asked me where my emergency family plan was, and of course it was done through the ASU [Area Support Unit] Toronto orderly room and never made it to the MFRC.

She really did not seem interested in looking into anything either, because she stated again that it was our fault that she didn't have it. Putting myself in her shoes, I would be a little more understanding, willing to discuss the situation with reference to the lack of information and seem to be a little more interested. She was not any of those things.

I also missed two meetings concerning the deployment for the family members. I asked her what those were about, and she said that they were information sessions. She said there was one woman there who had never done this before and she found it very helpful. So I told her that I had never done this before either, but got no response. It really felt like she just wasn't interested.

I could have gone over there, unlocked the doors and ordered pizza and accomplished the same thing that she did. Her husband was there with a video camera and had the kids record a message to their Dad. She handed me the tape (120 min tape) with the two messages from my kids and said, 'Here, mail this.' (Honest). I was disheartened but honestly not surprised. The other woman there didn't seem very thrilled either.

She also mentioned that the lack of information could be the social worker's fault. I told her that we didn't see a social worker before my husband left, and her response was, 'of course you did, everyone does!' We didn't—everything was very rushed so I got a call from the Padre instead. Which was fine with me anyway. Well here I am again complaining, but it just amazes me that this kind of stuff happens again and again. Maybe they should read their mission statement again. I told my neighbors that I feel I am getting more support from an ex-military wife from Petawawa whom I have never met than I do from the MFRC. Anyway, the children did enjoy their time there so I will take them to the next one and have a discussion with the deployment coordinator in the meanwhile. Maybe I am expecting too much! Thanks for letting me vent.

While I'm aware that there are two sides to every story, I suggested to the deployed member's wife that perhaps the lady in question was a civilian and not understanding of our lifestyle. To find out that she was a military wife and had been in the position for over a year was very disheartening. However, my own conversation with the same person on another issue left me feeling much the same as the complainant and again I was saddened that care and compassion seemed to be lacking. To have a deployment coordinator not make an honest effort to help a deployed member's family is inexcusable.

I've always found it to be a wonderful, creative, well-staffed group of people who grow and adapt to our community here in Edmonton. (I've been here since 1997.) I used to volunteer there with children's programs that I loved. I have only ever had one bad experience that I was able to put in perspective and move on from. However, today I learned of another circumstance, which is unsettling, and I'm quite sure it will be corrected but I thought I'd share it anyway. I had a lady just yesterday, mom of four (aged 2 to 10), DH deployed for the first time. She discovered a lump on her breast and, of course, ended up with an initial mammogram appointment the following day. After she and I both exhausted resources for childcare, we went to the Padre and got access to 'emergency childcare' to find out the evening before her appointment that she was only entitled to a three-hour window of childcare. I actually only found out about the MFRC response from the wonderful soul who was kind enough to pitch in and watch the kids at the last minute.

My question is this: shouldn't emergency childcare be emergency-oriented? I, for one, am almost completely unable to properly schedule my emergencies to fit a timeframe. I know the unit of the relevant member was handling it from the top down but, sheesh, what nonsense, I say. Obviously there are limits to such things, but really, a three-hour window? Rubbish!

A Different Kind of Support

Military personnel are such versatile people, wouldn't you agree? At present, the majority of the Army here in Britain is replacing the Firefighters who are on strike for more money, even though they get more than most of the soldiers who are covering for them. I was so proud watching our soldiers driving off in out-of-date military fire engines, going out to protect the public. Not once has a soldier complained! As usual, they have just got on with the job given to them to do.

Besides the support members of the military community provide to each other in various forms, our troops continually provide support to civilian communities. They go where they are needed. But each flood, hurricane or snowstorm they must deal with means more time spent away from their families. No doubt their help has been appreciated wherever it has been given, whether following the Ice Storm in Ottawa, the Red River floods in Winnipeg, the recent hurricane in Halifax, or elsewhere. Civilians should stop to think what helping them means in terms of the time a military member must give up being able to spend with his own family. The military lifestyle involves frequent separations and tremendous sacrifices on the part of the military members, their spouses and families.

Chapter 3

A Peaceful World—
UN/NATO *Tours*

In the civilian community when you lose a friend,
you mourn. In the military community when you lose
a friend, you wonder if your husband will be next.

I'm not from a military family but do want to say how proud I am of our Canadian peacekeepers and their families. I weep with you all when our media shows the general public the heart-wrenching goodbyes that must be said as new troops move out to serve in wartorn places. It certainly is true that 'they also serve who only stand and wait.' I too pray daily for peace.

Many years ago, another military wife and I spent a day manning a table display at our local shopping centre as part of a project. Her husband had been given next-to-no notice that he was to deploy to Bosnia and within a week he was gone. There wasn't the usual amount of time to prepare for his departure, and I knew she was really feeling his absence. I had invited her to my home on more than one occasion, but for the most part she just wanted to remain in her own surroundings. Shortly after her husband left, she was involved in a car accident that upset her even more. She was badly shaken but unhurt. Their car sustained considerable damage and this was a problem she had to deal with by herself. Knowing that this was an extremely rough time for her, I prepared a cold plate supper for her, and at the end of our day, I gave her the supper (in a cooler) and a hug. I know what it's like to be standing on your feet all day talking to people and how tiring it can be, and so I thought she'd appreciate being able to go home, kick off her shoes and just enjoy a prepared meal.

The following week when she came to my home to return my containers, she presented me with a beautiful piece of parchment paper on which was a saying that has meant so much to me over the years. So much so, that I've added it to my website, had it framed and given copies to several military wives who have had an impact on my life, and to some ladies who I felt just needed a little boost and who I knew would appreciate it: "No one knows how long the tradition has been observed—One Red Rose—handed from military wife to military wife and from friend to friend and always with love and deep appreciation for a welcome, a thank you, or merely a reminder that we all strive for the same goal. A Peaceful World."

Yes, a peaceful world. How we all wish for the same thing. Unfortunately for all of us, today's world climate seems to foster more unrest, more unhappiness, more greed and corruption, and above all, a greatly increased need for Canada's military to support the war on terrorism. With that increase come more demands of not only our troops but also of their families. Over the last 10 years, we've seen our troops off to Iran and Iraq, Somalia, Rwanda, Kosovo, Bosnia, and now Afghanistan—to name only a few of the out-of-country postings.

I'm sure everyone is well aware of our shrinking Canadian Forces, our inadequate equipment, and the Liberal government's lack of commitment to supporting our troops in the way they should and need to be supported. Far too many of our troops have had to serve on tour after tour after tour. In 1996, I had an occasion to discuss family life with a retired general who was on a fact-finding mission traveling from base to base. At that time, I felt our troops were being overworked and distinctly remember saying "You can't keep doing this (sending the same troops on tour over and over again) to our troops and their families." I'm sure that similar sentiments have been voiced time and time again by many—but who is listening?

When I first gave thought to this chapter and how I would present it, I struggled with some aspects of it. But thanks to so many of you ladies, you have really opened your hearts on the topic of tours. Your combined voices speak much louder than my voice alone ever could.

I just discovered your website today and it could not have come at a better time. I am faced again with the reality of the military and my husband's duty—he just returned from Afghanistan and is now leaving in

September for his third tour in Bosnia. I can tell you that the prospects of this tour have really made me struggle with my emotions, yet again, and with his leaving for the third tour since our daughter was born in 1998. Yet how do we say, 'don't go?' I can't. Anyway, I just wanted to drop you a line to say thank you for setting up this website. It is a gentle reminder that we are not alone in our feelings.

Messages like the one above make it very clear to me just how much military spouses need to connect with someone who understands, someone who is on the same emotional roller coaster they are riding. Just knowing that you are not alone can remove a tremendous weight from your heart. This mobile lifestyle tends to make us feel so alone at times in that our family support network is oftentimes thousands of miles away. As always, I answered this lady's message and offered a listening ear whenever she felt like reaching out to someone. I wanted her to know that I'd be there for her.

Hi Dianne. Thanks for taking the time to respond to my e-mail. I guess I could tell you for hours about my feelings. I agree that standing by and loving a person who is in the military is so important. Being married to a military man is first of all a very unique situation; I believe that you really do have to love that man! I often try to place myself in his shoes and know that it would be so difficult to leave family and, more than anyone, the children. The time they are absent is something that can't be given back [to a military member].

I understand from talking with my husband and others that there is a feeling that the pre-deployment stressors are vast, and the feeling seems to be 'don't let the army know,' despite their efforts to support the family unit. Military social workers don't hear the whole truth as it is, for 'fear' that if the truth were told the husband wouldn't be allowed to leave if the underlying issues were brought the military's attention during that pre-deployment phase. I myself am a social worker, and I get so frustrated with my husband's career; often I am left feeling like I will always come second in his life. I have come close in my mind to leaving, but haven't because I love him too much to ask him to choose. The army already places these guys in this position so often—family versus military duty. We all know the duty always wins.

I can tell you that I truly understand why military marriages oftentimes fail. These guys are so trained to control these emotions and feelings, that I think even if they are thinking or feeling something that may assist in keeping the marriage together, they are dumbfounded in how to communicate it to their partner. I often tell my husband that while he faces war, I myself battle a war. The army wants them to keep secrets and the wives want them to just talk! After all, it doesn't seem like too much to ask from the man who comes and goes, while we hold down the fort, and I truly believe that they just don't know how.

Secret to a good military marriage? No one knows. There isn't one as far as I am concerned. While other couples argue often about small things, military marriages are an ongoing battle to let go of someone you love, explain to the children why daddy has to leave, cope while he is away, and finally, get reacquainted with a new man each time he comes home. I believe that there is a special place in heaven for the military.

I am a military wife, with five children and another on the way. We are stationed here at Ft Carson, Colorado. My husband, who has been in the military for almost six years, will be deployed next week. At this time I am very scared, depressed and already feeling the loneliness and hardship of not only being alone with my five children, but also afraid of what may happen. There are so many friends and relatives that tell me not to think negatively, but it is hard not to think of the things that could happen and how I would tell my children. I try to push it aside but there are times when you have to ready your mind for these things. But until my husband returns home, I will pray and seek the Lord as a protector for every soldier that is leaving to serve our great country.

The following messages were contained in a military wives' e-mail group of which I was a member. The topic was the impending war in Iraq and who, if any, of our forces would be required to go:

I just turned on the radio and they are giving an hourly 'countdown to war' (Iraq). The feelings are so on-the-surface now. I want to cancel my plans for the evening and just stay home with my guy. I don't know what your 'guys' are feeling now, but I know that mine wants to do his duty and this scares the hell out of me. I don't honestly know what I would do if he wanted to sign a waiver, because he hasn't been back for a year yet. I am so wanting to go to Borden now, and get him in school for the next two years, either that or break his leg if he gets any crazy ideas.

Joe already said if they asked he'd sign it (the waiver) in a heartbeat and do whatever or go wherever was asked of him. Makes me mad as hell, but proud as hell at the same time. Damn!

George has also said that he wishes he were there. I just say that I don't understand, but would support him as per usual. I like your idea—break his legs!

OK, maybe I have the only soldier in the Canadian Armed Forces that has absolutely no desire to be in Iraq. As we watched the news last night, we were talking about Canadian involvement with humanitarian help when this is all over. Sandy heaved a huge sigh and said, 'I really don't want to have to go clean up someone else's mess.' I know if he was sent he would go, no excuses, but I think all that sand from Afghanistan has left a bitter taste in his mouth."

I really had to chuckle at the "break his legs" comments, as when we were a young military family and I was having difficulties dealing with John away so much, I often said that if they called him to war I'd break his legs so he wouldn't have to go. His response was that it would be a wasted effort, because they'd send him anyway!

Iraq—I have strange feelings about the whole thing! I know deep down that my government is right because they know things that we don't know about the whole Iraq situation. James just wants to go! He is watching his friends go and wants to be with them. He wants to be with the young lads on their first deployment to help them and to give his experience to them. He has always had this feeling that this is unfinished business. He was one of the first into Kuwait and he spent a lot of his time ahead of the front line.

Me? I want him to go for a few reasons: 1) It's what he has trained to do. 2) It would make him happier and less frustrated. 3) I want to be part of the crowd! Sounds strange? At the moment I am living on a garrison where

80 percent of the military have gone. I feel left out. Everyone tells me how lucky I am. I am supporting all the other wives and I don't fit in to a lot of their conversations and groups. At the moment, James goes away most weekends and for a few weeks at a time. In total he is away more than the other husbands are but just not in one go! If he could go away for six months I could get into a routine! 4) Family and non-military friends keep asking if he is going—I would like to shut them up by being able to say YES!

I know I mustn't complain, but it is hard playing the waiting game!

Dear Lord, where was this site three or four months ago? I am happier tonight than I have been since before Christmas, when we first got news of the tour to Afghanistan. Finally, someone is saying what I've been thinking to myself—where is the fairness in all this? What kind of life is this to try to lead? I'd like to know how I ended up in this situation, where my life is being managed by bureaucrats I don't know, and who know nothing of me or what they are asking.

The troops don't know how it is. They are over there with their friends, who are all going through the exact same thing, while I'm stuck here with people asking well-meant questions, or not understanding when you are starting to have a mental breakdown, if only for five minutes.

This tour is very difficult. At least during his tour to Bosnia in 2000, I could look forward to something—his R&R [rest and relaxation], the LTA [leave travel allowance] and an estimated homecoming—but now I feel like I'm stuck in a constant state of purgatory, with nothing to look forward to.

I'm frustrated, I'm angry, and I have nowhere to vent it. If one more person makes that condescending comment about how I chose this, I'll scream. I chose 'him,' not the army. He chose the army. I'm just paying for it, having moved from Newfoundland to Alberta, leaving all my family, friends and my natural support network, to sit in an empty apartment wishing he was here. Any sacrifice is worth being with him, but now I've sacrificed and he still isn't here, he isn't even safe.

I constantly wonder whether I've made the right decisions, or if I've let my love for him override my own good sense. As we aren't married yet, I've started to wonder if I would be better off cutting my losses and just leaving. I know it would break my heart, but I'd eventually be able to move on. As it is, I'm breaking my heart over and over with each new tour. Finally, I feel like someone out there understands.

Of course I responded to this lady's e-mail as I felt such compassion for her and certainly understood how alone she must have been feeling. I hoped that by our e-mail exchanges I could somehow make her feel just a little better knowing that someone was listening.

Thanks so much for your e-mail. I've been sitting up way too late, way too often lately, feeling miserable and sorry for myself. You see, I finished my degree last week. After 10 years of university, I've finally achieved my goal— I'm graduating from law school and I'm so deflated that Rodger isn't here to celebrate with me. He's been one of my biggest supporters since I got the idea in my mind about going back to school to pursue this degree, and all the way through my schooling. It doesn't seem fair that he's missing my graduation.

So now, I'm finished school, and I haven't found a job in Alberta yet, because I'm originally from Newfoundland, and left only to go to law school. But I didn't expect to fall in love with my friend in the army and decide to stay in Alberta permanently. Every time I go to a job interview, they want to know why I've decided to move to Alberta, and when they find out that my fiancé is in the military, they are afraid to give me the job because they think that he'll be transferred and they will have wasted all that time and money in training me.

I have a lot of time on my hands right now, and I'm driving myself crazy— so I thought I'd play around on the Internet and stumbled across your web page. Suddenly, I don't feel quite so alone. Thank you, thank you, and thank you. You can never know how much it's meant to me. Good night and God bless—and I'll be checking out some of those resources that you mentioned.

She and I exchanged more e-mails and I made a note of her graduation day and sent her my congratulations. Her parents were able to travel to Alberta to attend her graduation so she wasn't without family support on her special day. We eventually did meet when I was traveling to military bases conducting interviews. She is a lovely lady who has what it takes to make a good military wife and I was so glad that we got to exchange hugs!

• • •

On learning of the *HMCS Iroquois*'s imminent departure to the Gulf of Oman, I contacted my niece in Halifax to inquire whether her husband was still on the ship. He was due to leave with the ship but was returning after about eight weeks to fulfill another work-related commitment. I also chatted with other wives whose husbands were part of the ship's crew and I discussed the impending departure with the Director of the MFRC in Halifax. The following is a compilation of my notes on this stressful time:

As the *HMCS Iroquois* glided through Halifax Harbour on its way to the Gulf of Oman, family and friends remained on the jetty, watching their loved ones as they sailed into the open sea. *I watched the sail past and when I could no longer make out his facial features, I lost it.* Emotions, always close to the surface as families say goodbye one more time, sometimes just cannot be contained. *At one point in the sail past there was complete silence—it was eerie— then an older man shouted, 'We love you, God speed.' Through the crowd a child's voice was heard 'We love you Dad.' This prompted a happy little boy of about three to look up at his mother and immediately burst into tears.* Once more, military families called on their inner strength to help them get through another long separation.

With only 10 days' notice that the ship would be sailing, there wasn't much time for families to prepare for this important separation nor was that a normal preparation time to ready the ship. But what the public rarely takes into consideration are the tremendous organizational skills our military possesses. They were very evident during the Red River floods in Winnipeg several years ago when the 1st Battalion, The Royal Canadian Regiment was tasked to help with flood control. With vehicles and equipment already lined up on the parade square in Petawawa, ready to depart for an exercise in Gagetown, New Brunswick, the unit made a complete about-face, repacking vehicles and reorganizing well over several hundred personnel to help in this civil disaster—all within a few days

A deployment affects not only the spouse—it affects the whole family—and sometimes in ways we least expect. We need to keep strong lines of communication open with our children so that their fears, apprehensions and misconceptions are discussed and so that they can have a better understanding of why Daddy or Mommy is away and what they are doing.

Last night, after I had the boys tucked into bed, I sat down with a cup of tea and flicked through the channels. I stopped on CNN and watched hundreds, maybe even thousands, of troops saying goodbye to their

loved ones. Ken came around the corner from the kitchen and found me sitting in our living room with tears running down my face and asked me if I was OK.

My heart was breaking for each and every one of those families. Daddies saying goodbye to babies that were asleep in their mothers' arms, little boys and girls pleading for them not to go, but the one that really broke my heart was a nine-year-old girl with her infant sister on her lap. Her dad had just left to head to Iraq and her mum (a nurse reservist) is on 72 hrs' notice. She talked so maturely and seemed like the 'grown-up.'

It really had me thinking about how our kids do grow up faster in this lifestyle. They have so much more on their plates than the average civilian child. I think back to last Easter and the huge upset I had with my nine-year-old. He blamed me for sending his dad to Afghanistan. Just before Ken deployed, he came home with the usual papers for me to fill out. You know—the ones asking how you feel about the situation, if you have a support system in place, etc. My son had seen us filling out these papers and for four months thought I had signed his dad up for Afghanistan, and blamed me for his going.

As members of the military community know, everything is subject to change and that was never more evident than when a Sea King helicopter accident took place on the *Iroquois* only four days out to sea, requiring its return to port. On takeoff, the helicopter suddenly lost power and slammed back on deck, slightly injuring a few military personnel and causing damage to the helicopter itself.

The Halifax MFRC had only a 20-minute head start to notify 300 families about the accident before a media briefing was to be held. With a staff of 20 (and the availability of extra personnel if required) the MFRC activated its family call-out plan to notify the families of the ship's return and the reason for it.

One might think that the callers would be met with apprehension and panic from those family members they contacted, but instead their calls were met with sincere appreciation and calmness. Quite often the resilience, strength and firm resolve of military spouses are underestimated. Yes, life can be difficult and yes, the lifestyle resembles an emotional yoyo—up one minute and down the next, but life goes on regardless of the situation.

To ask a military spouse how she feels as she watches her husband depart is an insensitive question. Unless you live the lifestyle, it's extremely difficult to comprehend the magnitude of these abrupt life shifts. There is no question the sadness of the departure is there, the worry and concern for their partner's safety and the apprehension of the long, lonely months ahead, but spouses will tell you: "I don't want him to go, but it's his job—it's what he is trained to do and I support him."

Having just experienced the emotional yoyo in full swing, families of the *Iroquois* had a bit of a reprieve with the ship's return—but then they had to go through the whole emotional process all over again—and it's never easy saying goodbye the second time around. *It was very upsetting, I was just getting myself into a routine and then I was overjoyed at seeing him again, if only for a few days. But now he's gone again!* You want that one more day, one more hour, one more hug. You want to put off the inevitable.

With a normal six-month rotation and the usual lead time to prepare, some families find that they just want their partners to go and get it over with. *The sooner he goes, the sooner he'll be back.* But with less than two weeks to come to terms with not just another separation but one that has added worry and anxiety, saying goodbye takes on a different intensity. Many have heard "I don't know how you do it, I couldn't," from their civilian acquaintances, but what civilians don't understand is that you marry the man and take on the lifestyle. They are a package deal.

As one military wife put it, "Your friends become your family and your family becomes your friends." With families most often thousands of miles away, their support can be offered only from a distance. But the friends you make in the military lifestyle have all "been there and done that" and their support, especially at highly emotional times, can make the difference in coming to terms with all the challenges this lifestyle involves. Military spouses are the backbone of the Canadian Forces. They play an important supportive role—although they seldom get the recognition they deserve.

Canada, as a member of the G8 group of countries, has a responsibility to be involved with peacekeeping in other countries. We have always tried to help to bring about peace in other countries; this has been part of our makeup, and I don't think this is going to change in the near future. Yes, I agree, we are putting Canadian lives on the line for what seems to be a fight that is not of our concern, but believe me, we have one of the best-trained forces around. I live in Europe at this time and I know that

Canadians are well-respected and treated as equals among other G8 countries. I know that we may have poor equipment and poor pay, but compared to others we are doing just fine. Owing to Chapter 7 of the UN resolution, the peacekeeping role has changed over the past few years and I would prefer to say that our soldiers, airmen or sailors tend to go into the role as Peace Support, which allows them a greater role with more fire power. This [need] will not go away, and as more countries in the world struggle to find peace, I think Canada will always be a part of the process. I am proud of our airmen, sailors and soldiers, wherever they are. I know that they put up with hardship and see some awful things, but because of them, you get to live in the best country of all—Canada.

We have the ongoing problem of Northern Ireland. Even though the rest of the world thinks the peace process is a success [here], it is not. People still get hurt and we still have to watch our backs. At one time the terrorists would give us warning of a bomb—now they plant them in people's sandwich boxes!

War makes victims of us all. I am occasionally overwhelmed when I consider the ever-increasing numbers of families that get ripped apart by wars that are not of their own making. Sometimes it seems that none of us can escape the repercussions of war. What I don't understand is those who do not make any attempt whatsoever to put themselves in another person's place and make some effort to understand the horrific pain that comes when parts of a family must go and parts of a family must stay behind during and after wars.

I find myself coping better than I thought I would with my hubby gone. I realize that, 'Hey, I am doing this all on my own and surviving,' but now I find myself reflecting on the things that are out of my control. It upsets me to know all the little things he is missing as our baby is growing up. I know that there is never a good time for them to be gone, but it doesn't make it easier. I also miss sharing with him at the end of the day all the silly things that happened. I try to make up for it by writing as much as I can in letters to him, but it's just not the same. I know I 'picked my road' as everyone non-military likes to remind me, but I just needed to vent!

🇨🇦 *My DH (darling husband) called last night and it was really bad timing—right before the kids' bedtime and I was rather crabby. I felt so bad after I talked to him. Thankfully, he knows my moods and phoned back later. I know that I should be happy he called at all, but some days I just feel like my plate is completely full! He phoned to make sure I would remember to go for an oil change and tire rotation. Bless his heart! He's halfway around the globe and still concerned for us.*

Afghanistan

For a book to accurately represent life in the military community today, all facets of that life should be included and although the possibility of losing some of our soldiers is one that none of us wants to acknowledge, we must. Why? So that those who have died in service to their country will never be forgotten. But also to acknowledge the pain and suffering of those left behind, for they have paid the ultimate price as well.

When I designed my questionnaire, my thoughts often wandered to the tragedy of 9/11. That unforgettable day has caused all of us in the free world to stop and reflect on our families, our way of life and our relationships. For the first time in my life, fear crept into my thoughts. My world as I knew it had changed forever. No more would I, nor would most people, feel as safe and secure as we always had.

One thing I wanted to hear from those spouses who responded to the questionnaire was what their biggest fear was. After chatting with many ladies whose partners were involved in the first tour in Afghanistan, I realized that our fears for our partners' safety had increased 100 percent. As the completed questionnaires began to arrive, I noticed that most respondents had avoided noting their primary fear in answering that question. It was as though everyone felt that by not acknowledging the fear that a spouse or partner could be harmed, one could avoid worrying about that possibility. If you don't acknowledge a fear then you don't have to deal with it. However, acknowledged or otherwise, fears were soon realized, but not in a way we might have anticipated: Early on the morning of April 17, 2003, near Kandahar in Afghanistan, four CFB Edmonton-based soldiers were killed, and another eight were injured, when two US F-16 pilots dropped a 250-kg bomb on a group of

Canadians performing live-ammunition exercises on the ground. The pilots claimed that they thought they were being attacked. Regardless of one's thoughts on the friendly fire incident that took the lives of four airborne members of the 3rd Battalion, Princess Patricia's Canadian Light Infantry (3PPCLI) located in Edmonton, Alberta, and injured eight of their peers, the bottom line is that the reality of how quickly lives can be lost and families can be changed forever hit home with a powerful force.

When I first started traveling to military bases to chat with families, there was no question in my mind that Edmonton would be one of my first stops. The thoughts and feelings of many of the ladies from that base are contained in this chapter.

Edmonton

As I viewed messages sent within an e-mail group of military wives—many whose husbands were on that first tour to Afghanistan—I was humbled by the depth of their feelings and the compassion they showed. Nowhere in these messages was there anger towards the American pilots that caused the tragedy. Perhaps that came later for some, but the one thing on everyone's mind was not the cause of the tragedy but the fact that it happened. I share some of these ladies' responses with you because I know many of you expressed the same or similar thoughts. These messages show just how strong a bond there can be between military spouses:

My emotions have been all over the place today. I was woken up this morning by Steve's call at 6 a.m. saying that he was all right. I hadn't even heard the news yet. I was so relieved, then shocked. I have been through gratefulness that he is okay, sadness, anger, and now I think that I am just numb. This tragedy is so awful and I have no idea what to do.

My heart was broken when the news broke last night. At 0355 hrs, when I was told Ken was not involved, I had expected a form of relief but the emptiness was still there. I know my gratitude to the Lord will be forthcoming for this particular pass through the gauntlet. For now, however, the pain and anguish over the loss of these dedicated men is still real. I do not pretend to understand the loss of a partner, but the useless loss of a father, a brother and a son are all close to my heart and so it is my deepest empathy that I would like to extend to those of you here that were close to these soldiers. Please know if there is anything I can do to contribute or assist at this time, I would be honored to be there.

I have been at a total loss for words. The pain in my heart for those families and our men is so great right now, that it feels as if it could burst. I believe this has been the most difficult time I have faced in years. The waiting is almost enough to drive you mad. I am thanking God that Dean was able to call this morning. I also would like all of you to know that we are here for you if you need us. May God bless and sustain us all.

I finally heard from Darren this afternoon. He sounded very tired and upset. They had just had the memorial and parade for the soldiers that were killed. I'm so worried about what this will do to the morale of our troops. All I could tell him was how much I loved him and how proud I am of him. I sure hope this tour isn't longer than six months, because I don't know how much longer I can stand knowing he is in so much danger. I suppose I have deluded myself to the impossibility of his being hurt or killed. I think that's why I'm finding this so difficult; reality of it all has finally set in.

The first thing I did when I got home tonight (after kissing my kids) was to open this site. I feel totally empty. I still haven't spoken to Sam. Having been with the guy for 20 years, I could see such pain and anger and I cried with the need to hold him. I left yesterday at 6 a.m., flew to Ottawa and was picked up by the realtor who was beside herself with grief as well. She had totally changed our schedule and booked 15 houses for me to see that day (after 5 p.m.) I bought a house last night, did the inspection, lawyer and mortgage today and then took the red eye and got home here at midnight. I did not want to be away. It all seemed so unimportant. I am nauseous with pain. It is truly amazing how much better I feel being home and able to connect with people who understand how I'm feeling. We are a great bunch. I was reading the paper on the plane tonight and could feel tears pouring down my face and I didn't care who saw them! I will be at the family day tomorrow and beware because I have this need to hug everyone—this is just so, so sad...

When Peter called he was shaken and wracked with guilt that he was not there to help save his buddies. My toughest job is to just be here and listen to whatever he needs to say or share. It's easier to handle my own pain than his. Ladies, we need each other so very much right now. I've become so very close and connected to all of you in such a short time. It is so much like what our partners experience in their deep friendships during adversity. We're in our trench, so to speak, and relying on each other to survive.

I, like most of you, feel the tears are just there ready to let go. Am I the only one who really just wants their man to come home? I know he's gone for the entire tour—the likelihood of sending them home early is, well, next to none. But I just would love to be able to hold him so close right now and not let him go. Life is short and precious and we should be living each day to the absolute fullest. I love my man and miss him terribly. I know that with time, it will be easier to handle his being over there, but that doesn't make today all that much easier. I am so very grateful that he is okay and yet, I am overwhelmed with grief for people I have never really met, knowing it could just as easily have been my man. I really don't know how the families are coping; they are, by far much stronger than I know I would be. I pray that God will be with them in their time of need and that he will help us all accept our grieving and bring us closer for the support that we all need. I thank you for just being there, for not judging, for feeling the same fears, and the same loss. I thank you for just being the wonderful, supportive, understanding people that you are.

Today was gut-wrenching. I would love to have my husband home, if not for good then for a long, long hug. A few of us were saying, though, that it would be impossible to ever let them go again, so probably better that they don't get home until they are going to stay. I would be happy to just talk with him at this point. He called but spoke with my mother, as I wasn't back from Ottawa yet. She said he sounded very quiet and beaten up. Oh, I miss him so much. I sure hope we're talking July for when they return. I was very embarrassed with myself today—I couldn't seem to get a grip and stop crying at times. I am so glad that I wasn't judged by the wonderful folks who I know—you guys.

I just wanted to let you know how grateful I was for all of your listening and support today. I spoke with my hubby tonight and asked him if he has used the peer counseling or anything and of course he has not. How did I know that? I asked him if he thought perhaps he should, but he was very abrupt with me saying, 'I'm fine, just fine...everyone here is dealing with this just fine.' I know that he does not want me to worry. I am petrified that he will come back a broken man. He did sound better today than Thursday morning when he called. How do I know what to do or say? I don't want to push the issue. I wish I could just make it all go away like I do when I kiss my two-year-old's 'owies,' but I know how unrealistic that is. I feel so selfish, because I am happy that my husband is safe.

Thank you for putting all my feelings into words! That is all exactly how I feel. I worry so much that Shane, too, will come home a broken man. He has a difficult time showing or sharing his emotions at the best of times. Something like this could be detrimental. I also had no idea what to say to him about it all. All I could tell him is that I am here for him no matter what, and how proud I am of him. I think that is all we can do. There are no words that will take away the pain that our troops are feeling.

That's all I'm getting—the 'I'm fine, everything is fine' sort of responses. I talked to him tonight and we chatted about my new job and the arrangements that I've been making with regards to childcare, etc. He totally freaked out when I told him how much it would cost. Anyway, we got into a little skirmish on the line with regards to if I should even take the job or not. I think he is just afraid that I'll be working when he gets back and won't be able to take any time off. Justifiably, I'd like to wrap my arms around him and not let go for about a month! To make a long story short, we got off the phone and didn't say, "I love you." About 10 minutes later he called me back and said "I just wanted to say I love you, we may be going off to do something and I might not be able to call for a couple of days." All that I could say is OK be careful, I love you too.

Of course at this point in time, I'm a bundle of nerves as usual. I used to think of myself as a pretty tough cookie; I don't know what the heck happened to that posturing female who felt she always had to prove herself to everyone, but she sure as heck hasn't been around here for a while. Truth be told, I don't miss her though. I think I was probably meant to wear my heart on my sleeve. I feel more real, more honest somehow.

Dave finally phoned about an hour ago. At first I was so pleased to hear his voice and then I found myself so angry with him. What is wrong with me? Am I nuts? I crave to hold him, yet when I hear his voice I'm mad. That's it, maybe I am 'mad'… My Dad was in the military for 36 years and so my Mom knows the life, but they cannot relate to what is going on now. That is why I will be eternally grateful for having you all in my life.

I wanted to ask about what to say about the terrible thing that happened. I know Danny didn't know them well but he was on the exercise when it happened and I don't know what to say to him. I wish I could just take all his pain away, but I don't want to push for fear of upsetting him, especially when I know there are always other people around him and I know he worries about me and doesn't want to upset me here. It's a circle. He never wants to talk about it—he's worried about upsetting me but does he really understand that no matter how bad it is for me, it's worse for him? OHHH, I miss him so so much!

I sure wish I could have joined you all at the memorial and potluck today. Unfortunately, my son became ill yesterday and we spent the night in the Emergency Room trying to fight off a fever of over 104. Anyway, we are doing better today. I want to thank each and every one of you for your strength these last few days. We moved here nearly five years ago and it has been a real difficult go. There have been times when I have felt so out of touch with the whole 'army life.' It hasn't helped that I have always been an incredibly shy person. I was told a couple of years ago during one of my bouts of loneliness that to be shy is to be selfish, as God gives us each gifts to share with others. I don't know how many times I've reminded myself of this. You have all extended yourselves in such a beautiful way, that it seems only fitting to acknowledge what a tremendous bunch you are.

I felt that I had gone totally mad by Saturday morning and was comforted to know that everyone was feeling the same tremendous grief. I was at a total loss for words when Howard phoned me. What was the right thing to say? The best I could do was to tell him that I love him and was sorry for all of them. I *know that he has to shut down in order to do this job and come home safely to me, but how do I not share my deep pain with someone who has always been my best friend and confidant? I just ache right now, for him, myself, all of us. I have the utmost admiration for the military spouses that have been through multiple deployments and years of giving up their partners to their job.*

On a lighter note, I was so proud tonight when he called. My youngest said his first real clear word! I held the phone up to his ear and he laughed and said 'Daddy.' Howard was a little choked up after that, but was so pleased…

Hubby called me back at about 9 a.m. to wish me luck on my mid-term. I grilled him for more information with regards to his having to go do 'something' 'sometime.' He told me that no one was sure what was going on, he just wanted me to know that he loved me in case…. I feel like a weight has been lifted off me. I recognize that it is unreasonable for me to expect that he will stay in camp, safe in his sleeping bag for the rest of the tour, but part of me wishes for it all the same.

And from a stay-at-home husband whose wife was on tour:

On Tuesday, I went down to the Airport to see the rest of my Airborne brothers home, and they were looking good. I have been wearing Airborne colors since this happened, and will continue to do so until they are all buried. I don't grieve very well…. Losing people hurts. Seeing the strength you women have on this site makes me very proud to be associated with all of you. I thought being a paratrooper showed strength, but I see in all of you, an indescribable force that makes me well up with pride. I have now seen a side of women I never knew. Being back here is just like being at the pointy end of another type of spear. Thank you for showing me what courage and strength are all about. Trust me, facing bullets and landmines is a lot easier than facing emotions.

Lately I have had nothing but feelings of bitterness and disappointment. I know Alex is having a hard time. He's tired, has had enough and wants to come home. In essence he has become quite depressed, withdrawn and detached. He doesn't seem to e-mail anymore and hardly calls. I'm sure it's his way of coping and trying to stay focused. I just can't help but feel shut out. I am doing my best to be supportive, but am finding it difficult to stay strong lately. I have this overwhelming feeling of needing to be connected to him during these hard times, but he keeps pulling away. Are these normal reactions for him to be going through or is it going to be detrimental to our relationship when he comes home? I just don't know how to handle it all; this is my first tour.

I have noticed fewer e-mails from my hubby, too. I wonder if it is because they are busy. I know that on previous tours, he has stopped writing regularly because he says there is nothing he can tell me that isn't either classified or depressing. I have discussed this with him upon his return from tours; he says that it gets too depressing thinking about our wonderful life back home while he's living in a shit hole. For that reason he tries to throw himself into the 'there and now' and disconnect from life at home. It isn't/wasn't out of a lack of love or commitment to our life together—it was a coping mechanism on his part.

Me, I need e-mails. I am trying to sort out a move and getting little to no help from him. It must seem like a different world to him—back here. But it is important and real to me. The simple solution is that they have other things on their minds. I know my hubby doesn't want to burden me with his thoughts and feelings when he is feeling down because then I worry. So he doesn't tend to share it—trying to protect me. Perhaps your loving husband is trying to protect you. Things will be different once he goes through the re-integration process and settles back into real life. They have experienced things that no other Canadian has and they will have a bond to each other forever. I tell my hubby that he'll be a popular man at the Legion when he is 70! They'll be buying all of our guys drinks.

Hang in there. We are all here for you. I can't imagine what those guys are going through over there in that shit hole. My husband only likes to call late at night when the baby is sleeping because it makes his heart hurt when he hears him in the background.

As far as your relationship when he gets home, honestly, it's never easy. But what relationship is easy at the best of times? It's such a line to toe about getting them to open up, but still giving them their space (even though you want to be connected at the hip). It's tough, but you will do it.

Petawawa

In the spring of 2003, with rumors that the 3rd Battalion, The Royal Canadian Regiment (3RCR) would be tasked with a six-month tour in Afghanistan that summer, an uneasiness crept into the military community in Petawawa.

For my part, I just prayed that I could finish this book without having to deal with any injuries or loss of life from the 3RCR Battle Group. Why? Because I didn't want to see anyone else go through the pain experienced in Edmonton. Also, not only was Petawawa a community that was dealing with so many soldiers taking part in this current tour (as well as one in Bosnia), but many of those soldiers were from the same unit I worked for up until my retirement (1RCR). It's human nature to think that nothing is going to happen to you—only to someone else—but thinking that way provides only a false sense of security, as everyone is vulnerable. And now, with local troops gone and with constantly hearing the worries and concerns of so many, I couldn't bear the thoughts of having to deal with it. We all prayed that there would be no loss of life, but everyone was aware that it was always a possibility.

The first stressor for the local families occurred when a rocket attack took place in Kabul, Afghanistan, where some of our Canadian troops were stationed. One or two minor injuries occurred, but the impact on the families back home was tremendous. No longer could they keep their 'uneasy' feelings about this tour in the back of their minds. They finally had to give voice to their apprehension and fears.

One lady was at work in a store when news of the attack reached Petawawa. She was given the news by another military wife from her husband's unit, who came into the store and told her rockets had been fired into her husband's camp. *I was just numb. You'd think I'd break down crying, but all I wanted to do was get to a phone and call someone to see if the story was true.* A perfect example of a seasoned military wife—not believing everything she hears but attempting to verify what she had heard before she dealt with it. *He e-mailed me the next day and then I settled down. We have an understanding that if I don't get a phone call then everything is OK.*

With everyone on edge as this 'close call' was slowly accepted for what it was, some of the troops started to return home on leave from Afghanistan. Many wives will tell you that saying goodbye the second time around is much harder than the first—even though after the time home on leave, the remaining time in theatre is so much shorter. You just want to hold on tight and never let go.

One military wife described her feelings on her husband's return home, on leave from his tour in Afghanistan:

I'm home but I'm not—he's home but he's not. How confusing is that? Have I set high expectations for him and him for me? I am afraid to let go and relax, as I am concerned that when he goes back it will be that much harder to deal with the separation. The kids and I have come so far in these past two months, to have it messed up. I am just not sure I can do that. Yet, at the same time I want to enjoy my husband while he is at home. He is only home for a while, and I do not want him going back with my wishing I had done something different, because then it's too late.

When I was waiting at the airport, I had butterflies like you wouldn't believe. I walked in there and automatically looked for other military spouses waiting to pick up their husbands. I couldn't believe there was one lady I recognized. She was pleased to see a familiar face also, so we sat together, and waited, and waited. I got up a few times and paced the floor. That last half hour was the longest I have experienced in at least two months. The other was on the day my husband was to leave and I was waiting for them to form up and get on the bus. It is so hard to believe that it has been two months already. The feelings inside are still fresh or raw. I guess maybe that is why I am afraid to let go, as the kids and I are nicely getting into our routine, and are now at that calm point in this tour, a point where we can cope the best we can with things if they should arise, a point at which they are finally opening up to me about their dad being away. I am afraid that we will have to start all over. Does this sound selfish or what? I am so glad to have him home, my partner in life. But at the same time, I have my guard up, not wanting to get too comfortable.

His plane finally landed, and when I saw him walk through the doors, I could not believe my eyes, he looked so tired. But yet, I knew he was glad to be home. I slowly made my way through the crowd, and found him. I didn't even look at him; I automatically gave him the biggest hug I could give. Then as you can imagine, the tears of joy came rushing to the surface. It felt so good to hold him, finally to have him in my arms where HE IS SAFE. He whispered in my ear, 'I love you, baby, it's good to be home.' I will hold on to those words and treasure them every day.

The kids met us at the door when we got home or should I say the driveway. My daughter said she kept going back and forth to the door, and waiting out-side for us to return. My son was soon to follow. The smile on the children's faces when they saw their dad was amazing. They couldn't get enough of him. I had had my time with him and went and climbed in bed for the night, as I was so very tired from the drive. I did this to let the kids and their father spend a little time with each other. Before too long my husband also came to bed. We lay together, and just took in the precious moments of finally being together again. I was having a hard time realizing that he was home, and at the same time struggling with the fact that HE DOES HAVE TO GO BACK. I think this is the biggest challenge I am encountering at this point in the tour.

The first challenge was for the children and me to make it through this spe-cific tour. I knew we were going to have to work even harder to communicate, and be aware of each other's feelings. This tour is just so different from the others. This one has a higher risk factor, bringing with it different emotions that we hadn't experienced before. As my husband and I talked in bed, he commented that he, too, was pleased he was home, and also he wasn't. So here we are, both with the same feelings. Both of us know how the other is feeling—which helps us to get through the adjustment period. After a few moments passed, he had fallen asleep on my shoulder and there I was looking up into the darkened room, wide awake, with thoughts swimming around in my head, 'How do I relax and make the most of his time at home?' By now it is 3 a.m., and I can't seem to get to sleep. As I sit here recording my thoughts, I have watery eyes along with the feelings of joy and calmness that he is finally home.

During her husband's leave, the tragedy of October 2, 2003, occurred: Just as they were getting used to being together as a family again, their emotions, along with all of ours, were ripped wide open when word was received that two members of 3RCR, Cpl Robbie Beerenfenger and Sgt Robert Short, were killed, and several others were injured as the Iltis vehicle they were driving in was shattered by a mine in Afghanistan. I was unprepared for the emotional force that hit me. All of a sudden, our whole community was experiencing first-hand what the military families in Edmonton had faced 18 months earlier. At the time, my husband and I had guests visiting from England. The man is in the British Army and he and his wife live on a military base in Britain. This tragedy struck a chord in their hearts as they had just dealt with the loss of several military policemen from their base that were murdered in Iraq. What all of us had feared had become a reality.

News quickly spread—not only throughout the base here at Petawawa, but nationally as well. Once again, we were preparing to acknowledge Canada's loss. Our families here now echoed the emotions contained in the paragraphs from the ladies in Edmonton. What this recent tragedy also did was to reopen wounds, not quite healed, of our peers in Edmonton. It was an extremely rough time for all in the national military community. My thoughts were so deep that it was not a time for me to take pen to paper. I couldn't record my thoughts—I just needed to deal with them and understand them.

As I sat waiting for the funeral service for Cpl Beerenfenger to start, I glanced to my right, to another seating area arranged in curved rows, and the impact of seeing a whole row of non commissioned members, resplendent in their dress uniforms with most bearing five or six medals on their chests was amazingly powerful.

My next thought was that they don't have room for any more medals! Then I suddenly realized that any or all of them could be my children. They were so young to have experienced so much! If they already had a chest full of medals and were only half way through their career, what did the future hold for them?

My thoughts then wandered to what each of those medals represented—to them and to their partners. For the service member, each medal represented time away from family, a commitment to our country, and living in harsh conditions those of us at home could not fully comprehend. They represented the dedication of each and every soldier to follow orders and, despite being overworked, use outdated and inadequate equipment, to do the best they possibly could. Those medals represented the best that Canada had to offer. They represented pride in our country and pride in themselves. They had earned every one of them.

But I couldn't help but think how many more tours these young Canadians would have to endure before they couldn't take it anymore, before they left the lifestyle behind them—whether in retirement or in disillusionment. When the chest becomes heavy with medals, so does the heart—for all that has been missed, for all that has been lost, for all that shouldn't have been.

As I scanned the crowd and looked at the tremendous support for Rob

Beerenfenger and his family, my thoughts turned to what those medals meant to the spouses, the ones left behind. They represented loneliness, fear, apprehension, worry, and enough tears to fill an ocean. The medals represented months and years of living apart from your friend, your partner, your lover, and your husband. They represented being strong, capable and supportive. They represented the biggest sacrifice a wife can make—sharing her husband with his country, many times taking second place in her partner's life.

While each medal pinned on his chest is a mark of pride to a military member, to his spouse it is a reminder of the effects that each tour has had on him. Those medals represent an anxiety in each wife's heart over whether their relationship can ever get back to the way it was. Will it be better or will it be worse? It's certain it won't be exactly the same. And for Mrs. Beerenfenger and Mrs. Short, who also lost her husband, and all the other wives who now must carry on alone, those medals represent the ultimate sacrifice. These special, supportive ladies have given until they can't give any more. They've lost forever what mattered to them most.

During the time around the friendly-fire tragedy, my computer system was infected with a virus that left me unable to get into my website. I felt frustrated that I could not acknowledge this devastating time through my website, as I knew people would be visiting the site for just that reason. And so, when our soldiers in Petawawa were lost, I was determined to put all else aside and create a condolence page. I felt it would be an avenue for people outside our geographical area to express their feelings to the families who were suffering so much. I was utterly amazed at the hundreds of people who responded and was very touched by so many messages that came straight from their hearts:

I feel terribly sorry for the wives and families of these two soldiers who passed away in Afghanistan last week. I hope everyone somehow manages to come to grips with this. This is the one sad part of a soldier's life that is a reality that some of us have to face. But at the same time, we are so very proud of our spouses, out there protecting our country and us. We live in a great place and we cannot forget that. —Military wife in Petawawa, Ontario

As a person married to a soldier currently serving in Afghanistan and who served in Rwanda, Bosnia and Somalia, I am always filled with fear and feelings of uncertainty with each tour and am so sorry this fear

has become a reality for you and for so many Canadian families in the last few years. Every time an accident happens, I thank my lucky stars I have been spared 'this time' but am truly so sorry that you are feeling the pain that we all pray we never have to experience. —Military wife in Petawawa, Ontario

Be proud of your husbands. Canadian soldiers and their families are the strongest people on earth. —Wife and daughters, sister-in-law and nieces of two soldiers serving in Afghanistan (Petawawa, Ontario)

Our thoughts and prayers go to those who have fallen, and our thoughts and prayers go to those still standing. I am glad that all Canadian soldiers wear the uniform proudly. These wives and families need to keep their heads held high. We are all very proud of your loved ones. Thank you for standing by such great men. God bless all those who are in need at this time. —A wife who has a loved one in Bosnia

WAR IS HELL! Having served beside soldiers as these and been trained by fathers of our young heroes, I feel such a great sense of pride not only for the different regiments that are tasked to serve but for the thousands of people that daily put their lives and families on hold so the rest of us can sleep like babies in our beds at night. Canada has but a small role in this battle but the job we do is tremendous, and with huge consequence. My heartfelt pride and sorrow go out to the wives and children of the families that have fallen members and the families that are missing the cornerstones of their lives as I too have been separated from my wife and children for 22 months but get to see yet another day. —PRO PATRIA X 3RCR Edmonton, Alberta

We cannot know the impact of October 2nd on the families involved, we cannot imagine the sacrifices made by the families of the fallen men and we cannot heal the hearts broken by this tragedy. We can continue to support each other and never forget the ultimate sacrifice made by these men and their families. On behalf of my husband, currently serving in Afghanistan, and my family, our heartfelt condolences. —Military wife in Petawawa, Ontario

I can only imagine the pain that you are experiencing. I know that words will not ease that pain but hopefully with time your broken

98

hearts will mend. My husband is also currently serving in Afghanistan, and even though there are times when I don't understand why they are there, he truly believes that they are making a difference. When he told me about this terrible tragedy, I could hear the sadness in his voice. I can only pass on to you my heartfelt sympathies. In times like these, it saddens me to think of the sacrifice that you, your husbands and fathers have made. I like to believe that they died trying to make this world a safer place where little children can grow up to be happy and free. —Military wife in Deep River, Ontario

I guess it does not matter whether we have met or not, only that we are bound together because our loved one chose to serve his country. When one spouse, child, or mother feels pain and loss, believe that we are there beside you feeling pain and loss as well. Your courage to stand tall in this time of need serves to remind us how precious life is. My family would like to pass on condolences to the families who lost a loved one. Tonight I will whisper a quiet thank you to your husbands for serving their country well. —Anonymous

No words can ever express the sympathy we have for you and your children. Your loss is greatly felt by the entire country but primarily by military wives. May God hold your hand at this horrific time in your life and envelope you in His love. Please know that our hearts go out to you and that my tears are flowing as I type this. Having gone through my husband's four tours, I know you are living every military wife's worst nightmare. I have read all the letters of condolence so far and they all sound the same. That is because our sentiments all come from the same place—the heart of the Canadian Military. God bless you and your children. —Military family in North Bay, Ontario

My heart goes out to you, my thoughts and prayers are with you. As a military wife and having experienced the loss of a loved one, I know that no words spoken could ever erase the pain you are feeling. Please know that there are families, a community and a nation who grieve with you and a God who will support you. This will help ease the pain. We offer you our love and support. May God be with you. —Military wife whose husband is deployed to Afghanistan

🇨🇦 *When death and loss grip us and squeeze every last drop of tears, we realize all who go there are chancing death. Whether I agree or not as to why they went to war is not important. But I do agree that they (people at the top making the decisions) are not giving them all of what they need to assure their safety. Even though I have been out of the service for thirty years, upon finding out how some have lost their lives brings me to tears. Now being a civilian I no longer have to start at the bottom and work my way up! I am going to the top! I am going to mail letters (continually) until they realize that you can't say the loss is a casualty of war when it is the under-equipped or uninformed that die. I too wish they all could come home in one piece.*
—*Ex-Sailor in Halifax, Nova Scotia*

Seeing their partners off after their leave at home following these tragic deaths took on a much stronger intensity. To let go one more time was almost unbearable.

🇨🇦 *Larry went back to Afghanistan yesterday afternoon. It was pretty tough emotionally. I am afraid even though I would have liked to have said something really profound to him and shared that I loved him, I couldn't even look him in the eye. The pain was so great. I was afraid the waterworks would come and I wouldn't be able to stop them.*

I have to say sending him back the second time has been excruciating at times. I have a friend who was in such turmoil afterwards, within a few days she had booked a flight home to her mother country. Another leaves in January for hers. So I know I have company in my pain and don't feel like there is something wrong with me.

Only hours after sending him off, I felt that edge of the unknown. There is a fine line between fear and hurt. I know I have no control over his safety, but I still fear for it. I am desperate to somehow make it safer or better for him. It is probably that mothering instinct.... I feel like I'm on a deathwatch and I can't shake it. I don't think I could handle another tour.

My heart hurts and I cannot make it stop. I need to cry, but I can't. I know I am holding my breath again, but I cannot ever really exhale. It's like when you cut yourself and you catch your breath waiting to see how bad it is. I am waiting to see how bad this will be, and when I get the all clear, I'll let myself breathe normally again.

While the Afghanistan tours have been the main focus of this chapter because they are current and both have produced casualties, we must not forget our troops serving in other countries and the many other military families who have paid the ultimate price and have grieved the loss of a spouse.

Currently, more troops from Petawawa are serving in Bosnia and many spouses echo one wife's comments:

I have been feeling that some people have been looking down on the tour to Bosnia. I get the feeling they almost think it is not as valuable as the other (Afghanistan). I understand that it is not as dangerous, but the fact remains that we are all without the ones we love, they are not at home, and it is dangerous!

We must also offer a special prayer for the families of those whose partners are flying on our Sea King helicopters. The stress and apprehension they must deal with every time one of these helicopters takes to the air is tremendous—not to mention those who must fly in them. One has to ask, why? Why are the politicians not acknowledging that we are in a crisis situation with these buckets of bolts?

Since the tragedy in Afghanistan on October 2, 2003, measures have been taken to rethink the use of the Iltis vehicle in which the deceased and injured men were traveling. Measures are now being taken to give the Army some new equipment for these tours. And yet they are still arguing what constitutes proper equipment. The bottom line is, listen to the soldiers. They are the ones who know what is required—not the decision makers sitting in their safe, secure, comfortable offices in Ottawa. Families of those on the front lines would sleep easier if they knew that these military members could receive the appropriate equipment to carry out their jobs.

Why did it take the death of two dedicated soldiers, husbands, fathers, sons, brothers and nephews to create a scurry in Ottawa to purchase new equipment? Although the government has committed to buying new equipment, by the time that equipment is due to arrive, a new government—perhaps with different priorities—will be in place.

Is the order for this new equipment going to fall to the bottom of the same ocean in which the cancelled contract for EH-101 helicopters (to replace the Sea Kings) now sits? The same ocean in which the leaking submarines recently purchased from Britain might end up? Many military spouses are afraid of the answers to these questions.

The Soldiers Left Behind

Much is said and written about our troops who go off on tour, but not as much is mentioned about those who stay behind. Those who must pull up the slack for the missing members. Those who haven't stayed behind by choice but because there are needs to fill at home as well as away.

The following story was created by a lineman's wife for a new website for the Canadian Association of Forces Linemen. Two weeks after the article appeared on the website, the web editor was instructed by the president of the association to remove it from the site because it was questioning the policies of the Canadian Forces.

On the Road Again! How much is a lineman worth?

It is the Labor Day weekend and school starts this week. Parents across the country are looking forward to the first day of school, but not in this house. The same day our son starts back at school his Dad will be on the road again for the next 39 days.

I know you all are thinking this is the price you pay for having a husband in the military and a lineman no less! Other wives have to put up with their husbands being gone six months at a time, and still others say their farewells for three months. For a myriad of reasons the wives are [constantly] saying goodbye to their husbands and living the life of a married, single parent.

When I listen to the news and I hear that the boys are coming back from this tour or that one, the only thing that I can think is I WISH!

I wish my husband were gone once every two years for six months at a time, earning extra money with that UN pay and coming home for a three-week holiday during that time away. I wish because then I would see him more often.

Since February my husband has been home exactly 136 days. I won't see him for the entire month of September and part of October, so in total for this year alone he will have been gone 175 days (that is if they don't send him anywhere else when he returns). But it doesn't stop there; we start this all over again in January after the Christmas Holidays.

This kind of schedule will continue until he's posted to his next unit (approximately two to three years). What is worse, he doesn't get paid like the rest of the military who are away from their families, there is no UN pay or separation pay or even spec [specialist] pay. They get enough money for food and lodgings and that is it.

One hundred and seventy five days, in which my partner has missed out on award dinners, graduations, birthdays, and even our wedding anniversary. I get tired of doing everything by myself, grocery shopping, mowing the lawn, taking care of the house, and taking care of our child. People assume things when your husband is never around, sometimes they even think that you're not married and sometimes they think that you have to be cheating on your husband because he is gone so much. People can think what they want, but it's when they tell me what they think that it hurts.

I would probably be able to accept that he is gone this much if there was some money in it for us, or the chance of an award or else a medal, but there isn't. He may be serving his country, but serving doesn't mean slavery. Some of the military likes to compare their workforce with the civilian workforce and truthfully there is no comparison. In the line trade at this moment they are so under-staffed and have so much work to do that if an entire crew got sick and they were ordered to take time off, they would have no one to replace them; the work would have to wait until they got better.

In the civilian world, not only would you be able to find a replacement crew but you would also pay them overtime to get the job done on time. Not our boys—if a job has to be completed and they are behind schedule, then they work late, no extra pay, no appreciation for doing the late hours, and sometimes no time off before or after the fact. They just can't afford to take time off, considering the workload and the staffing problem.

In the civilian world, you can only have a person work so many hours before overtime kicks in and they get extra money for working holidays; my husband can't even save up his holiday time, let alone get paid extra.

In the military world, if a man makes the decision to go to work on his holidays to complete his reports and finish his paper work then he does that and no one even shows their appreciation until PER [Personnel Evaluation Report] time. In the civilian world, you'd either be told to go home or promoted within six months. Not the military—you have to wait two years to even be considered to get your name on the list.

The military makes rules and gives excuses, but the facts still remain the same: there is too much work, too little pay and too few people to do the work. The men are supposed to be able to have two days off prior to leaving for a road job and two days after, but that is at the Commanding Officer's discretion, and if there is work or training to do, well the priority goes to the work. I would have liked to have had my husband home for a couple of days before and after just for the sake of getting the house in order prior to leaving and just to unwind when he gets back. But as things are, it can't be done!

These are the facts of life for a lineman's wife and nothing I say here will change a thing that the military does. I just wish that while they are sitting in their offices thinking up the next great excuse of why they can't pay linemen (052) spec pay that they remember one thing—if you have no one to lead you have no empire to build!! Think about it!

Spec pay may not help very much, all things considered. The men will still be on the road, working late hours, never getting any time off or appreciation, no separation pay or UN pay, but maybe with the spec pay you could attract some new linemen into the trade. Maybe with spec pay a husband being gone on the road all the time wouldn't be so bad; at least he'd be getting paid what he's really worth.

I know this sounds as though I am a bitter wife who doesn't appreciate my husband's service to his country, but I beg to differ on that as well. I am a patriotic Canadian; I love my country and the freedom that comes with being a Canadian. I just don't think that it is fair that the linemen get so little, for doing so much. It is time they did the right thing for the linemen and that means all of them. If you have difficulty with the concept, just ask yourself: how much is a lineman worth?

🇨🇦 *I am very proud of my husband, I know he's an awesome family man, and I believe in his career choice. I know he is the type of guy the army can use and they will make full use of his potential. When he is home, we make full use of it, the boys cling to him (and so do I) and keep telling each other that this is hard, but it will not last forever and that our family will be stronger because of it. I don't even want to think of the alternative, so I choose to believe....*

Chapter 4

Life Goes On

*This lifestyle has made me the person I am
today and I'm very happy in my own skin.*

Life is not always as we would like it to be and this holds true no matter what lifestyle you lead. Recently I asked several spouses what they had learned about themselves since joining the military lifestyle. The following are some of their answers:

I have learned that…

… I can take a lot more than I thought I could. I can do a lot more than I thought I could on my own. And I have learned of a new level of love that I have for my husband that I didn't even know could be achieved.

… I have a lot of inner strength and am good at making friends even though I thought it was difficult. I've also become less judgmental of people.

… I love being a dependent wife. I depend on my husband for love and support, as well as food and shelter. Our lives are complete and I wouldn't change a thing. I loved staying home with our boys and being there when all three of them came home from their days at school and work.

… I am a very patriotic person. I love this country and I'm willing to share my husband so that all of us may continue to live in a free and democratic nation. I am also a very proud person, of my husband, of our country and all we do. I, too, have learned that I'm capable of a greater and deeper love for my husband than I thought possible.

… I'm damn tough!

... I am fully capable of caring for my children and myself. I am independent and yet never alone. Even when my husband is away, which is more than he is home, I know that I am well and truly loved. I am a lucky person, as I put no conditions on my love.

... Life is what you make of it, and sitting around crying my eyes out in loneliness isn't going to change the fact that my husband has a firm and passionate commitment to his country as well as to his family, and sometimes we have to share.

... I have been challenged beyond what I could dream I'd be capable of doing and I am very proud of myself for not only coming out of my shell, but also excelling—something I was always too shy and insecure to ever think possible. This lifestyle has made me the person I am today and I'm very happy in my own skin.

Many spouses have told me that they are somewhat frustrated with others' lack of understanding of their lifestyle and, in particular, their role in the military lifestyle. Yet just as many will talk about their frustrations with people who automatically feel we turn to a blubbering mass of jelly as soon as our husbands are gone. That we are quite capable of managing on our own—often accomplishing things beyond even our own expectations—sometimes remains unacknowledged.

In one of my classes we are a pretty tight-knit group of about 20 and we all speak freely. Most know of my lifestyle and are very respectful, but yesterday the one loudmouth in the class started blabbing how we are 'only a peacekeeping nation' like that's not an accomplishment or something! That just got the ball rolling and the next thing I know they are all joking around about how small and under-funded our military is. Thank goodness my professor saw my anger/disgust and ended the conversation quickly. But let's face it, they just don't understand.

Reading the following comments from a military wife in Britain will be a real eye-opener to many, and all of us maintaining a military home in Canada should be so grateful that we do not have the same stresses to deal with as our peers in Britain:

Because we live in a garrison, my husband can go to and from work in his uniform. But he cannot go anywhere else in it. If he lived out of the garrison he would have to commute to work in civilian clothing and change once at work.

We tend not to mention our situation to people we do not know. When things are at a difficult stage we will check under our cars for anything suspicious attached. Every garrison household has a special mirror on a stick to do this!

We always vary our routes to and from work, so as not to set a pattern that potential terrorists could use. We are not allowed to go to Southern Ireland on holiday. Our photos and names do not appear together.

Most of this stems from the Northern Ireland situation. It is not as bad as it was five years ago, but could always re-ignite and put us at risk. Also this is good practice for the present situation. It seems that this new breed of martyr terrorist is not concerned about its own welfare or staying alive and would therefore not give any warnings like the IRA did (the only reason the Irish terrorists ever give warnings is to give themselves enough time to get away).

In the recent months we have all been more aware of who is out and about. If a car stops for a few minutes outside your house you make a mental note of its make and number. As for phone calls, we never ever give out any personal information over the phone.

It all depends on what your husband does do and has done in the course of duty. Military personnel have been targeted whilst off work and the less you give away to strangers the better. Our garrison is an open garrison but in the event of a threat all the barriers at the end of the roads are brought down and armed guards are placed there. Many garrisons are 'behind the wire' which is safer for everyone but you are not part of the civilian community.

All correspondence is shredded and our telephone numbers are not listed. I am more at risk than other wives due to the nature of some of my husband's [previous] postings. If we were posted to Northern Ireland there would be many more restrictions placed on me. For example: You cannot use taxis over there, as many have been hijacked in the past by terrorists, you have a plan of places you can and cannot go; much of Belfast is off limits for us. Certain shops cannot be used and if you go for a girls' weekend off to the coast you have to lie to locals about who you are!

We have experienced a lot of 'home horrors' over the years. I remember as a child, bombs going off all over the UK. We never went into city centres at

Christmas, as on many occasions these were the terrorists' targets. My dad just missed being killed in the Birmingham Pub Bombings in 1974. He had just left a pub when it blew up. I was only a few months old...

I, like so many, am also dealing with a house, children, job, and husband away. When I married my husband, I was military, he was military and I had been an air force brat to begin with. I thought that whenever he went away it would be no problem because I grew up that way. I didn't stop to think about the difference between my father leaving and my husband leaving. I have since left the military and am trying my best to deal with the day-to-day catastrophes that inevitably occur.

I have not been offered any support by the base here. (I am in Kingston.) In fact, the most support I have gotten is from the other members who were not deployed, but as someone mentioned there are constant worries about rumors regarding the intentions. But really—the Quality of Life guys are not going to come here and shovel my driveway, they aren't going to change the oil in my car and make sure my reports are done for work. And they will not be here at night when my 2-year-old daughter and 4-year-old son are crying for their father while I have to explain, 'this is just what daddy does.'

This afternoon a woman (not military-affiliated) from my children's daycare was telling me about how stressful her week was—her husband had been away for four days and wasn't coming back until tomorrow. I just smiled.

I love my husband and he loves what he does. It is a big part of WHO he is and it is our way of life. Sometimes I wish he would find a civilian job and leave the whole thing behind. But then I think, who is to say he won't travel as a civilian. There are stresses in a civilian job that you don't have with the military such as 'downsizing' and 'cutbacks.' I don't necessarily believe that life would be better or less stressful as a civilian family—just different.

I am glad that someone is providing a forum where spouses can express their feelings and opinions on our unique way of life.

My husband was in the Canadian Military for 25 years. I don't know about other military wives, but even when my husband was at home he spent a great deal of his time at the messes as did many of the other soldiers I knew, while their wives stayed at home. Alcoholism seems to be another *problem the wives have to deal with a lot of the time. Or they can't show their feelings. It is lonely when they are home as well as [when they are] on tour.*

I am so proud to be a member of our military community and to serve others in our community. I remember being a young mother and new to the military culture...what a shock—but what a ride it has been! My husband has served in every element and is just finishing a three-and-one-half-year posting to the **HMCS** Montreal. *Each experience we have had, from Cyprus to Somalia, to living in Wainwright, Alberta, to city life in Halifax, has given me strength, taught me more about life than any other experience could have...I love it, I hate it, I'm sometimes ambivalent...but I love my husband dearly and at the end of the day that is all that counts.*

I moved here from Halifax, Nova Scotia, where I met the most amazing man, and flew from a community where I knew people and had family to a city where I know no one, and when he went away for three weeks, it was the most painful experience of my life. It is nice to know that there is a (web) page where I can express my feelings. Thank you.

I am proud of him and what he does and I have to remember that when I get frustrated with being the one having to deal with things here in the house, at work, etc., and being all alone, with nothing going wrong until he leaves, it's still harder for him. Last January, my dear hubby got into an accident with my car the day before he left on course for 2 1/2 months. That left me with no car for almost a month (in Winnipeg in the winter no less).

I think I am finding it so frustrating because I cannot call him whenever I feel like talking to him. I have to wait for him to call me. I tried to tell him how frustrating that is, but I don't think he understands. And it never fails that he calls as soon as I go out! Also, I have a real problem with my in-laws. They basically act like I don't exist—so when he is not home, they never call me to see how I am doing. I never heard from them all summer until I finally called them last weekend and then she made me feel like I was bothering her because I wasn't calling because something was wrong or something important had happened with her son.

When he went on his first tour, it was me who put them on the MFRC mailing list, and mailed them the map of Bosnia—they never even acknowledged or thanked me for that. My husband says family doesn't have to say thank you to family members for things they do (huh?). I just have to remember that it is hard for him to be away from home just as it is hard for me to be left behind. We did have a bit of a breakthrough—when he finally understood why I wanted to go to Alberta to see him rather than him coming home for his days off. I don't get to go anywhere, he always gets to see something new, do something different (okay, it was only Wainwright). But I think he finally got it that sometimes I NEED a break from home and a vacation away! It's so important to keep those lines of communication open, isn't it Dianne? You and your husband obviously have found the way to success after so many years together. I congratulate you and appreciate all the advice you can give!

The Bumper Sticker

Having been a supporter of military spouses at every opportunity for quite a few years, I was excited to find a bumper sticker that read: "Toughest job in the military—military wife!" It's certainly what I had been advocating all along and suited my sense of humor. I managed to purchase a few at a dollar a piece and set about sticking one on my car as well as the front of my desk. As I worked in an open area, the sticker was certainly viewed by many in the run of a day.

Reactions ranged from a few chuckles, quiet smiles and heads nodding in agreement, to my being asked where someone could purchase one. Only a small number had been printed, and they were grabbed up rather quickly; soon I was receiving orders that I filled from the small supply I had—at no charge. I was only too happy to see some of these men interested in taking a sticker home to their wives. It definitely told me something very positive about them.

After a couple of years, I received new office furniture and my desk ended up being used by the female sergeant in another department. She wasn't a military wife, but she didn't find the sticker offensive and wasn't inclined to remove it—that is until she received a complaint from one of her staff. In today's "politically correct" society, some people appear hell-bent on taking the word "harassment" to the extreme. Rather than make a fuss over the complaint, she quietly removed the sticker. It was some time later before I noticed it was gone and was flabbergasted that ANYONE in the military community would find this sticker offensive! It was ludicrous. I didn't ask who the complainant was, as I didn't need to know, and I doubt whether she would have told me in any case. But I just couldn't let the matter drop there. And so, I posted the story on my website and want to share some of the responses with you:

The bumper sticker probably could have stayed; who was it really hurting? The 'sense of humor' left about eight or nine years ago when the feminist females demanded to be everywhere. I say this, as I was a serving member myself and am of the belief that some trades should still be men only. Harassment is never a good thing, but it seems there is no room anymore for innocent jokes!

Soldiers offended by such a sticker clearly do not understand what a military spouse endures, let alone do they pass the 'well adjusted' test. In particular, I would hope that a person who is charged with defending the country would not try to explain to me that they were 'humiliated, belittled or embarrassed' by such a bumper sticker. By the standard of 'reasonable person,' it is only those of fragile self-worth who could possibly take offence. Is it not time we ask people to 'grow up'? It is a shame the quartermaster is unable to issue a dose of maturity and common sense to these soldiers of questionable judgment. Perhaps things would work more smoothly and some of our problems would cease, if only there was a NATO stock number available.

I'm so sad that the bumper sticker had to be removed. As a web-designer I know that several interesting colors mixed together produce a dull gray blah. So it is sad to see the same effect happening in our society. As we nobly strive for 'equality,' we lose the specialness that each one of us has inside. I do think we have carried things too far. I'm not in the least bit offended by holes in the road being called 'manholes.' I appreciate a gentleman who holds a door for me just as I would hold it for him if I were there first. Why do we have to replace common courtesy with clamoring for 'our rights?' Why can't we keep a sense of humor while we achieve our special status as 'unique' individuals who are all the very same shade of blah?

A few years ago my husband worked for a major corporation in Ontario. One day a male supervisor wrote a memo to his technical crew. As his crew was an all-male crew, he addressed his memo: 'Gentlemen' and proceeded to photocopy the memo. Accidentally, he left the original in the copy machine where it was found by a female technician from another crew.

The memo was not intended for her. She filed a grievance and won her action! How is that possible when the message was not intended for her, did not contain sexist or off-color remarks, and did not use foul language? Her complaint was only that the memo was addressed to "Gentlemen." I think that this type of overreacting has damaged the so-called women's movement irreparably. —Military Brat

One has to be extremely thin-skinned, and, as such, I wonder if suited to military life, to find such an innocuous statement 'offensive.' One might disagree with the statement, might pass comment to the pilot of the so-adorned desk, but to go through channels to get the sticker removed depicts to me a degree of personal insecurity worthy of further investigation by the authority so approached.

I would have told the complainant something to the effect that 'If you can't take a joke you shouldn't have joined' or 'Anyone is entitled to their opinion; you can post that your job is the toughest in the army, and see if anyone complains.' I do not mean to say that the sticker is a joke but that such matters should be treated in the good spirit in which they are intended: as a booster, maintainer of morale for the one posting the sticker and a conversation piece at most for others.

Had I been the Commanding Officer who received the complaint, I would have been more concerned about the well-being of the complainant than the political correctness of the sticker. But one might say that was in the old days, before common sense had to give way to political correctness.

Note: The Commanding Officer did not receive the complaint—it didn't go beyond the Sergeant who occupied the desk that the bore the sticker.

I can't believe the childishness of some people. How could anyone be offended by that bumper sticker? I have one on my car. If we remove humor from our day we'll all be very boring.

I am a military wife whose husband is infantry. We have friends from all branches of the military, each one (in fun of course) saying that they have the hardest job in the military. We all have a good laugh and then get on with our lives. No offense is taken; everyone realizes it's all in fun. How was that bumper sticker any different? We've all seen a lot worse! Maybe we should all worry about 'real' harassment in the workplace and find our sense of humor again. It makes what can be a tough life, a little easier.

A Potpourri of Observations

A Canadian military wife on a posting to England, offers another perspective on what's important:

Recently, 20 new Canadian families have arrived here and it is nice getting together with the wives to chat. We can blow off steam and whine and complain to our heart's content without offending anyone. The Canadian way of life is different from life here in Britain and we have been accused of being spoiled.

I think, on the whole, that Canadians are bigger consumers than UK people. We have more things (microwaves, multiple TVs, etc.) than the Brits do and I think that is due to the fact that our cost of living is cheaper. Without a military subsidy for utilities, we couldn't afford to live here. When I first arrived in the UK, the high prices of everything really bothered me and I promised that I wouldn't complain about high prices again when I get home. Yeah right!! I also wondered how people survived here with low wages and high costs. Now I know they survive by not having as many material goods as we do.

A lot of people in this area aren't well-traveled, so they haven't been to Canada to see how we live. The locals have no concept of the space we have and of the diversity of our country. I have been asked if we have daylight, do we have snow all the time. People are under the impression that we live in ice and snow continually.

Living here is also an education because at times I think that I am learning another language. I have had so much fun laughing at myself for the silly mistakes I have made. My favorite one happened when I was out driving around one night. I decided to turn around in the car park (parking lot) of a sports center not far from my house. I looked up on the fence and saw a sign that said 'No coaches beyond this point.' I sat there for about three minutes (or more!) wondering why coaches couldn't go on the field with the teams. I finally figured out they meant buses! Boy, did I feel foolish, but it still makes me chuckle over a year later when I think of that.

All in all, life here has been good and I am grateful for the opportunity to be here and live in another culture. Life overseas makes me really thankful that I am Canadian and [makes me] appreciate all that I have as a Canadian. I wouldn't change it for anything.

I have been married for 10 years now and therefore this is not by any means my first six-month period alone with my kids. But I must say that it never gets easier; military wives just adjust and get on with life and deal with it.

The issue of his being gone has been a hard one on both my husband and me. Mostly when I first moved here to be with him, there were a LOT of fights. Now I am more aware of my feelings on the subject, (the need to understand why he had to or wanted to leave). I try to rationalize my strong feelings or anger by keeping a positive attitude instead of attacking him and fighting about it. We still have our arguments, but I feel that we are making progress. I rely on my military-wife friends to keep me busy or to chat with so that I am not home alone thinking about how much I miss him. I really feel blessed by all the wonderful people who have come into my life since joining my husband here at his posting.

My husband tells me that I am a very special person to be able to put up with his job. But I don't feel like that at all. I feel like I'm just doing what I have to do to be with the man I love. However, I do think that it takes someone special to handle this lifestyle and believe that I do fit in that category, considering. His job in the military won't be forever, so I try to think of that when I miss him a lot or if he just got home and is leaving again.

I hope someone else reads this too; it may bring light to new military wives who are still trying to understand the lifestyle and may feel like they are starting to resent it or wondering if they can handle it for the remainder of his years in the military.

I wanted to let you know that I totally understand your situation. Ted and I were married in Sept 1992, and three weeks later he was off to

Cornwallis. *I should have taken this as a sign of things to come! Well, after he graduated he was home for maybe three more weeks before he left (without me) for his 3's [trades training course] in Kingston. When housing became available almost two months later, I left a career and nice apartment in Halifax to join him. I literally cried when I saw our place in Kingston (yup— the old concrete things—eeewww!). I supervised the move at both ends (not bad for a novice), and kept my cool when the movers 'accidentally' broke my car window as they unloaded it off the truck, in spite of the fact that a NASTY snowstorm was blowing across the lake and heading right for us!*

He was gone all day and spent most nights in study groups or at the school working on his Morse code. I was alone, in a crappy home, away from everyone and everything I knew, and I hated him for taking me away from them. It was winter, so it was hard to meet new people. It got a little better once I found work— it kept my mind busy. We moved to British Columbia after he graduated, but the real shock to the system came in 1996 when we moved to Ottawa. This time I had a one-year-old baby, and a month after we moved in, he was off to ALERT, of all the godforsaken places. I'd never had to care for her alone, and to be honest I was used to having him around. I cried every night for weeks. But like all of us, I found the 'stuff' to get through it. I'm lucky...so far he hasn't had to go away for really long deployments. Mind you, for two springs in a row I got to shovel snow in Ottawa while he went down to Puerto Rico and Florida with the fleet (ahem) 'on exercise.'

I don't know how we do it—both as a family and as military wives. We just do. And as you said—this lifestyle isn't forever. My mother-in-law is a (retired) navy wife from the 'old school'...25+ years on submarines and surface ships. If she can manage, I know there's hope for our generation! Without intending to sound too melodramatic here, I must admit that I've grown a lot since Kingston. I still hate it (and sometimes him) when he has to go away, especially when I've had one of those days when everything goes wrong. But you get past it. We've been married 10 years now (to each other AND the CF). It does get easier. Like the old saying goes: bloom where you're planted.

 I do identify with sometimes still hating it and him for leaving me here to deal with everything on my own, and coming home to an empty house and having to shovel my own driveway or mow my own lawn. But, I try to understand that this is what he has wanted to do since he was in

public school. So I try to calm the butterflies in my stomach and say, 'Sure honey, I'll be fine. You go on that tour...'

One of the advantages of using the Internet is having the ability to express your feelings instantly to anyone, anywhere in the world. That not enough people take the time to acknowledge or show their appreciation is made up for by the generosity of those who take the time to do so. It's obvious that the following comments were heartfelt, and my sincere thanks go out to Leslie Doolittle of Oklahoma for sharing her feelings with all of us:

Thank you for giving me the opportunity to express my support to the wives of the American soldiers. As the wife of a former US Marine, I sometimes experience a certain amount of guilt associated with the discharge of my husband. He was discharged from the USMC [United States Marine Corps] a year ago. A few months ago he expressed his desire to return to the MC (it's just in his blood). Being pregnant, we agreed to wait until after the birth of our child.

As the impending war approached and then got well underway, I couldn't help but tell him how glad I was that we had waited. I found myself just blurting out to him how I would be devastated and would never make it if he would have re-enlisted and left us. But, I began to think about the passion that I observed when he spoke of returning to the military, and with pain in my heart and a lump in my throat, I gave him the OK to do what he felt he had to do. Reluctantly (a reluctance out of fear) I told him I'd always be by his side and that I was the strongest woman in the world when it came to doing what I had to do (Lord knows I'm not).

I eventually concluded with encouragement. I encouraged him to do what he loved and desired to do, but inside I was nauseous. I know that in the blink of an eye my life could change and I could become a military wife. Just the thought of it scares me to death. But knowing that I would not go through that pain alone is my comfort. As is knowing that the untouchable strength that undeniably carries a soldier's wife through her days of lonely pain is the same strength that lies dormant within myself, and the same strength that allowed me (with a lump in my throat and a sick feeling in my stomach) to encourage the man that I love...with a smile on my face.

American Woman
By Leslie Doolittle

I woke up this morning (with you on my mind). I made myself a hot cup of coffee with two sugars and a little vanilla creamer. When I opened my blinds the sun came sparkling through the glass. Then, I drove our baby boy to his wonderful daycare center. I watched him smile in my rear-view mirror and I smiled back (with you on my mind).

When I returned home I sat down in my favorite chair (my rocking chair) and watched my favorite morning show, while I sipped on my coffee. I looked around at my cluttered house and began to plan out today's routine (with you on my mind).

As I was loading the dishwasher, I began to think about my husband. To me he is the most wonderful man in this world. His eyes light up a room. And his ability to love, along with his calm demeanor, is enviable to those who are even the most passive among us. I thought of how he is truly my hero (but of course, you were on my mind).

Today I couldn't seem to fight back the tears or the pain I felt when I thought of facing this world without my husband by my side. Women lose their husbands to their country every day and carry on; I honestly don't think I could. I suppose there is an inner strength that lies somewhere deep in a woman's soul. A strength that is so strong, it lies in wait for the right moment.

The wives of the military are an inspiration to the women of America. The Woman's Woman. The backbones of our country. The hearts of our Nation. The backbone and heart of the men who fight for America. The wives of the military are the eyes and minds that make certain their soldiers never lose concept of the America that awaits their return.

Now, more than ever, are the women of America strong enough to carry the weight of this great nation. Now, more than ever, I feel proud to be an American woman. The strength of the US military is a reflection of the women that support it. The wife of a soldier is a title of honor, strength and pride. Always remember that no matter what my day consists of—you are on my mind.

I can think of no better way to end this chapter than by including Colonel Steve Arrington's heartfelt thoughts as he took pen to paper. As I've stated many times, military spouses are the same the world over. We all go through the same emotions in this challenging lifestyle, and Colonel Arrington's comments not only confirm my statement but demonstrate an understanding of our role that is sincerely appreciated by all.

Military Spouses—There's a Difference
By Col Steven Arrington, United States Air Force (USAF)

Over the years, I've talked a lot about military spouses…how special they are and the price they pay for freedom, too. The funny thing about it is most military spouses don't consider themselves different from other spouses. They do what they have to do, bound together not by blood or merely friendship, but with a shared spirit whose origin is in the very essence of what love truly is. Is there truly a difference? I think there is. You have to decide for yourself.

Other spouses get married and look forward to building equity in a home and putting down family roots. Military spouses get married and know they'll live in base housing or rent, and their roots must be short so they can be transplanted frequently.

Other spouses decorate a home with flair and personality, the enjoyment of which will last a long time. Military spouses decorate a home with flair tempered with the knowledge that no two base houses have the same-sized windows or same-sized rooms. Curtains have to be flexible and multiple sets are a plus. Furniture must fit like puzzle pieces!

Other spouses have living rooms that are immaculate and seldom used. Military spouses have immaculate living room/dining room combos. The coffee table got a scratch or two moving from Germany, but it still looks pretty good.

Other spouses say goodbye to their spouse for a business trip and know they won't see them for a week. They are lonely, but can survive. Military spouses say goodbye to their deploying spouse and know they won't see them for months or, for a remote, a year. They are lonely, but will survive.

Other spouses get used to saying 'hello' to friends they see all the time. Military spouses get used to saying 'good-bye' to friends made over the last two years.

Other spouses worry about whether their child will be class president next year. Military spouses worry about whether their child will be accepted in yet another new school next year and whether that school will be the worst in the city again.

Other spouses can count on spouse participation in special events such as birthdays, anniversaries, concerts, football games, graduation, and even the birth of a child. Military spouses only count on each other, because they realize that the Flag has to come first if freedom is to survive. It has to be that way.

Other spouses put up yellow ribbons when the troops are imperiled across the globe and take them down when the troops come home. Military spouses wear yellow ribbons around their hearts and they never go away.

Other spouses worry about being late for Mom's Thanksgiving dinner. Military spouses worry about getting back from Japan in time for Dad's funeral.

And other spouses are touched by the television program showing an elderly lady putting a card down in front of a long, black wall that has names on it. The card simply says "Happy Birthday, Sweetheart. You would have been sixty today." A military spouse is the lady with the card. And the wall is the Vietnam Memorial.

I would never say military spouses are better or worse than other spouses are. But I will say there is a difference. Our country asks more of military spouses than is asked of other spouses. Military spouses pay just as high a price for freedom as do their active-duty husbands or wives. Perhaps the price they pay is even higher. Dying in service to our country isn't near as hard as loving someone who has died in service to our country, and having to live without them.

God bless our military spouses for all they freely give!

Chapter 5

Media

*Rumors (and the media's mighty pen) are the
Canadian Forces' worst enemy and can be more
deadly than any person pointing a rifle at me.*

With the increase and intensity of military tours to wartorn countries comes more visibility through various forms of the media. As spouses normally play a supporting role and remain in the background, the focus has not been on us, but rather on our partners who are carrying out various missions abroad. But that focus is slowly shifting.

Over the past 10 years, I have had the good fortune to speak with many reporters and interviewers. For the most part, I have found them keenly interested in our lifestyle. Their interest has been very evident in the questions they've asked. You can easily tell when a reporter has done his or her homework before an interview. You can also quickly tell when the interview is "just another assign-ment" to be finished quickly so that he or she can move on to the next one.

Over the years, I have always been treated with respect by the media and I appreciate immensely the coverage they have given my various projects and me. For the most part, I have thoroughly enjoyed my interviews. However, there were one or two reporters who approached our interview with a negative mindset. They were biased in their approach, and that doesn't sit well with me or anyone else in the military community who senses that negativity.

These biased reporters are the ones that cause many women in the military community to shy away from any connection with the media. They are also the ones who make it that much harder for good, honest reporters to do their job because, unfortunately, we seem to paint them all with the same brush.

When your emotions are on super-alert and you have no experience dealing with the media, it can be hard to determine what type of interview you're doing until you are in the middle of it. Because of the nature of interviews, there is no time to pause and consider questions before an answer is expected and many times, you might not express yourself as well as you would like to—emotions just get in the way.

For most military spouses, talking with the media is a new experience. It wasn't that many years ago that our thoughts and opinions were not solicited. The focus has always been mainly on our partners. But that has changed. Spouses are more willing to speak their minds today; they are more comfortable with having their comments recorded. And it is a step in the right direction that members of the media are now seeking us out and asking for our opinions—because we do have them.

I am still contacted quite often by members of the media who hope that I can connect them with some of today's military spouses. I made a vow at the beginning of my adventure in supporting military spouses that I would never pass on contact information without a person's consent. And so when I am approached by the media, if I am comfortable with what they are proposing to do, I ask for *their* contact information and am only too happy to pass it on to those ladies in the military community that I think might be interested in chatting with them.

However, there have been times when I've cautioned reporters not to expect much in the way of a response. "Once bitten twice shy" really applies because military spouses certainly have been "bitten" by the media and can be very quick to "close ranks" against them. When I give a few quick examples to media requesting contact information, of how some of their ranks have mistreated some of my peers, many are quick to reassure me that they are not like that. And I acknowledge that they are just trying to do their job—many times with impossible deadlines. But that doesn't change the fact that some ladies have paid dearly for their 15 minutes of fame as this following story shows. As the military wife in question learned, word of mouth can be a great advertiser or a very quick way to "shut the door."

Hard up and lonely: There's no life like it

On November 2, 1998, an article appeared in the *Toronto Globe and Mail* that greatly angered many in the military community. Written by a Social Policy

Reporter, this article put such a negative slant not only on our lifestyle but on the unsuspecting military wife who agreed to an interview, that it had a profound effect on the entire military community.

The young military wife whose husband was in Bosnia agreed to do an interview in her home. Little did she know the repercussions of her comments or the anguish she would suffer. Once the story was repeated in the Petawawa base newspaper, the buzz was fast and furious. I telephoned this young lady after the article appeared locally because I felt perhaps she could use a friend. But, I was a stranger to her and at this point she was understandably leery of everyone she didn't know. She didn't trust anyone. Things had gotten so bad that she was reluctant to shop for groceries because people were approaching her to react to her comments; her husband was upset with her and she was thinking seriously of traveling to Nova Scotia to stay with family until her husband returned. She was just miserable, claiming she had been misquoted—but to what extent I don't really know.

The article painted a dreary picture of our lifestyle, from "dun-colored houses in near-treeless yards" (and this was before the huge windstorm of a few years ago that knocked down over one thousand mature trees in Petawawa), "cramped military housing," "sleepy community," "meager pay," "featureless houses like cardboard cutouts," and the journalist's reference to the South Side PMQs as the "ghetto—with peeling paint and old drafty windows." The writer also described the wonderful tributes to military spouses sandblasted on boulders in Home Fires Park as "rings a bit hollow."

One had only to read the first few paragraphs of this article to know where it was heading. But what really upset the military wife who was interviewed, as well as many others (myself included), was the personal attack on the hostess who was good enough to invite this reporter into her home. She described the wedding picture hanging proudly on the wall: "the groom proudly decked out in his beige formal army uniform, the bride staring into his eyes and wearing a borrowed wedding dress at least a size too big."

I was appalled at the audacity of this woman to attack this young wife so viciously. When I spoke to the military wife she said: "I will never be able to look at my wedding picture the same [way] again," and I sensed she was close to tears. No doubt she'd already cried a bucket over this whole, sad experience. After all, what did her wedding picture have to do with doing an interview about a wife dealing with her husband gone on tour for six months? Absolutely nothing.

Not surprisingly, reporters had a very difficult time connecting with military spouses—particularly in this area—after the dust had settled on this issue. There was quite a public outcry and the *Petawawa Base Post* was flooded with letters to the editor. The newspaper received so many that it ran responses for several issues and was unable to print all that had been received.

My reaction to this whole experience was one of anger at the reporter, disappointment at the military spouse over some of her comments (if she was quoted accurately), and a need to respond to this whole issue. The following are excerpts from my reply, which appeared in the *Petawawa Base Post*. I include them here because I think military spouses can gain a lot by reading them and absorbing some of the advice. I hope this will help them in the future should they be approached by the media, and I hope the media reading this will have a better understanding of why they have perhaps met some resistance in trying to connect with spouses.

Having had some experience with various forms of media, I'd like to offer the following suggestions to any of the young wives who agree to do interviews:

- Be wary of reporters who do not live near a military base because they may not have a sufficient understanding of our lifestyle.
- Do some research of your own before you do the interview. Check on the interviewer—try and find out what type of reporting they usually do—are they usually positive, controversial, or does their reporting normally have a negative slant?
- You are not compelled to do the interview in your home. Pick another location if you feel more comfortable with that.
- Just because a question is asked doesn't mean you have to answer it. Stick with what you know.
- Be prepared for the repercussions that might surface after your interview becomes public. You have no control over what the end result of your interview will be.
- If you don't like the way the interview is going, then stop it.

The following story is a perfect example of the inexperience of many when dealing with the media. It was the young lady's very first interview and as usual, no questions were given ahead of time, as the media always prefers to receive spontaneous responses. Following the interview of two military wives who were friends, one became rather upset. She was worried that she had said some things she shouldn't have and wasn't comfortable with how she had responded to some of the questions. (Her husband was on tour at the time.) Her friend who had suggested she be interviewed was also upset and wished she hadn't asked her since the interview had obviously caused her anxiety. Shortly afterwards, the wife who was upset telephoned the person who had conducted the TV interview and requested that the portions she was uncomfortable with not be included in what was to air on the news that evening. Lucky for her, they hadn't planned on using the comments she was so upset about. However, had this been a slightly different set of circumstances, the reporter could have easily tried to delve into why the lady was so reluctant to have her comments become public knowledge. The fact that she wanted to "take back" some of her comments would normally pique a reporter's interest.

When we discussed this whole situation, the wife who had invited her friend to participate in the interview stated, "Well the military didn't tell us what to say!" I was completely floored at this mindset. It was as if it was another opportunity to blame the military and not put responsibility where it belonged. I chuckle at the thought of the military telling military wives what to say in response to any queries by the media. Undoubtedly, there have been times when the powers that be no doubt would have been happier if some comments by wives had not been made. But can you imagine the field day the media would have if there was even a hint of censorship by DND? Can you imagine how the wives would react if there was an attempt to censor them?

So ladies, think twice before you say yes to dealing with the media. Make sure you are comfortable with the idea and prepared to respond quickly to questions asked. When you are in the public eye, you are representing us all, and military spouses can be quick to voice their displeasure when they feel that they have not been accurately portrayed. By all means speak your mind, but do so knowing you are responsible for what you say and you must be prepared to stand behind your comments. Having said that, and having done some reporting myself, I know that all reporting is open to interpretation and the spin a reporter might put on an article presents his or her own perception of the interview. It might not always be the spin you intended. We are all human, each with our own reasoning and comprehension.

Over the years I've been misquoted at times, and sometimes a point I was trying to make in an interview was misinterpreted, but reporting is like medicine—it's not an exact science. All we can hope for is that the interviewer will have as much integrity and honesty as we do.

Living the military lifestyle is like taking an endless ride on an emotional roller coaster. Most civilians don't understand our lifestyle and certainly many in the media don't. We hope that they are genuinely interested in learning more about us through their interviews, but I'd like to offer some advice to those who are interested only in sensationalist reporting: There is nothing that turns a military spouse off the media quicker than having a microphone stuck in her face and being bombarded with questions that have been designed to bring her to tears. We've all seen reports on television that try to not only catch the emotional aspect of saying goodbye but—as we see it—to portray military spouses as a blubbering mess of tears. Yes, there certainly are tears—how could there not be when you are saying goodbye to your partner, your lover, your best friend as he or she heads off to deal with the unknown? These emotional farewells are part of people's private lives and should not be intruded upon by the media.

I remember watching one on-site interview in which it was obvious that the female reporter had no idea of our lifestyle. She openly admitted she didn't know how we did it (how many times have we heard that ladies?) and her relentless rapid-fire questions were designed to start the flow of tears. But the military wife she was chatting with had obviously been in the lifestyle for a few years and wasn't having any part of letting her emotions show. I remember sitting there saying to myself, "Good for you! You're not giving her what she wants." This lady calmly replied to her questions and basically said, "Yes, I'll miss him but life goes on" and it truly does. We don't crumble into a heap and remain there until our partners return. Instead, we do crumble a little (but mostly in private) and then we pick up the pieces and get on with our lives. We are more capable and independent than most expect of us. We are the backbone of the military family, we hold it all together.

Another irritant is being asked, "How do you feel?" That question, when asked by the media, is a complete turnoff. How do you think military spouses feel when they are being separated from their partners; when the reality that their partners are sailing or flying into God knows what kind of danger has just hit home? How do you think they feel sharing their partner with the world when they just want him by their side, home and safe? Don't ask that question—particularly when couples are saying goodbye. Emotions are just too raw. The best time to ask that question, if you must, is halfway through the tour when the spouses have had a chance to accept that he is gone, have gotten themselves into a routine that they are comfortable with—maybe then they can give you an honest answer. Because by then a spouse has her emotions under control. They are still close to the surface, but she is more apt to share her feelings with you at that time.

And so, to members of the media reading this chapter, if you want to get some good interviews from military spouses, here is a bit of advice for you. Do your homework, try to understand us, acknowledge the important role we play in the military community. Accept that we are on an emotional roller coaster a great deal of the time. Don't play on that, because if you do, then you'll find the walls going up and future access to military spouses will become harder and harder to obtain. Word spreads quickly and we do look out for our own.

We are a select group of women who love men who happen to have chosen the military as their careers. They put their lives on the line for all of us. Respect that. And the bottom line is, treat us as you would like to be treated. Your interview might depend on it.

Chapter 6

Dear Rose

... Oh, I can't wait for him to come home.
Do I tell him I hate the military?

My website has prompted many e-mail messages of thanks and support but it has also prompted women to share their stories and seek advice. Sometimes it's easier to unburden to a faceless stranger—and although I never set myself up as "Dear Dianne," I have been perceived as such by some. My approach to all e-mails I receive is to answer every one. If people have taken the time to contact me, then it's just a courtesy to return their e-mail. However, sometimes it has meant a week or so of really giving my response a great deal of thought before I send it. I am not an expert on anything—just someone who has lived the military lifestyle and has regularly stayed in touch even after my husband's retirement.

What makes it very difficult to answer some of these messages, like the two stories below, is that I can read between the lines and see that perhaps a relationship is about to end when the writers themselves either don't see it coming or are looking to have someone reinforce their state of denial. They are looking for someone to tell them everything will be all right. However, it's not for me to say one way or the other. You really can't get an honest feel for a relationship from just a few paragraphs in an e-mail message and that makes responding very difficult for me. In the end, the truth will come to light as it did in these cases, but these ladies need to find it out for themselves—however painful it is.

February 24

I don't know if I can be included in this tribute to all the men and husbands serving in Kosovo, but I thought that it couldn't hurt to try. My love of two years is leaving as we speak to Camp Bondsteel in Kosovo for the second time. He last served six months there as an MP [Military Police] patrolling the wartorn streets and miraculously returned home to see me at Christmas time. I am a student at a college in Florida and we have been through so much together. When I discovered that he was to be deployed again, I planned an emergency vacation to Wurzburg, Germany for two and a half days to celebrate our Valentine's together. I am so at a loss because all of the web pages are for wives and people with children, yet Carl and I are only 19 and 20, and he has three and a half years left to serve. Eventually we plan to be together, but so much is at stake with me still in college and our futures still unknown.

He is my best friend and if there is anything you can advise me about, it would be appreciated beyond understanding. I don't know how much longer I can take all this without him and I am so scared for him over there that there is no one who understands my situation. The four months to come are going to be more difficult than the first six.

Wow, we can all relate to this lady as we've all "been there, done that." Our American counterparts have had to deal with much longer separations than we have, and yet being apart from your partner for any length of time is the biggest single stressor for all of us.

In Sheri's next message sent to me the following day, she said:

February 25

Dear Dianne,

Thank you so very much for your wise words of advice. Yes, I do quite often send him care packages that relate to the season and one of my favorite pastimes is to buy him new clothes since he IS a guy and sometimes they don't always have the best fashion sense…and of course it is nice for him to wear something other than those BDUs [battle dress uniforms] all the time. Every day I send e-mails but he can only check periodically via the military's computers and his time is limited. In Germany, however, he has ICQ the chat program and is better about communication. My only qualms lie in the fact that being the Colonel's driver in the PMO [Project Manager's Office] for the next four months will place him in times of idleness and solitude. Before he had all his buddies there and we both get so depressed when there isn't much action around us. I am not as concerned for his safety as I was before (but mind you before I was a walking worrywart) but this is only because I think that I realize four months isn't as lengthy as six and that he is there with the Colonel so I know that special attention will be given.

You are right in your words when you say that over the past year we haven't been together, but as strange as this may sound I believe in my heart that we are closer than we have ever been before. I just returned from Germany and in seeing him there we had the 'talk' about marriage and our stances on children and the whole shebang I guess you could say. However that is not to say that we are planning anything rash or sudden. My goal is to finish school before I EVER get into a marriage and this means at least another 4-5 years since I will be attending grad school immediately after my undergraduate studies. Next March he will be able to return to the States—who is to say where?

April 3

Dear Dianne,

Thank you SO much for the e-mail. You don't even know what a horrible day I have had. I just got finished crying home to my Mom and waking her up at midnight with all my college life problems.... So to get you caught up on the latest with my man over in Kosovo.

February 17th he sent me tickets for Valentine's Day for the weekend to go see him in Germany. I was psyched! I had been to Germany before on a trip around Europe but had never traveled alone, much less done it all in one weekend. I left that afternoon, only missed two classes and came back the following Sunday. I had exactly 58 hours to spend with him, and another 24 hours were spent flying over there, not counting layovers. You could say that I was extremely tired when I got home, and had jet lag for at least three weeks if that is possible. Now that I think about it, I can't believe I was actually there!

It snowed the entire time, and I went from laying out on South Beach in

85-degree weather to 22 degrees and hail! *(I had never seen snow before.) I don't think I could ever fill anyone in on all the details of our trip, but it was jam-packed with our adventures. We drove to Amsterdam one day, went to a very nice restaurant...all Germans there, and had a picnic in the snow on top of the castle in Wurzburg near the Rhine River. Before I knew it, it was time to leave.*

And, yes, now I am fully back into the swing of this semester...it is almost over. And I haven't spoken with him in six weeks. The communication is very limited and I send him at least two e-mails a day for support. He tries to get one in here and there, but I guess it is tough since he drives the Colonel around every day. In June, he will get back to Wurzburg and I will be done with classes until August. I think we are planning another trip between those dates, if they give him two weeks off like the last time he came back from deployment. If it is a long exodus then I think he will come to the States, but otherwise I will go back!

It just gets really hard at times without him. We are free to date other people if we want to, but I know I don't and that he hasn't for months. I think that since we are best friends and have been together all through high school, that we will always be there for each other. But the other day I wrote him a letter that mentioned 'I hold him back from his duty' and 'I will never understand what he has been through,' and that type of thing. Major issues that we should talk about are normally NOT brought up via e-mail with him, but this subject I just can't stop thinking about. Does he really need me there? Or do I just make things worse? I hate never really knowing how he feels since his e-mails are so short and there is no time.

I am sorry this is so lengthy, but I am extremely happy that you still care! Thank you so much for everything, you really cheered me up. I will keep you posted on the latest if there is any word from him. Again, thank you.

June 8

I wanted to write you a super long e-mail about my boyfriend and I since things look like they have taken a turn for the worse. You see, he came home for a one-week emergency leave to visit his grandfather who was in the hospital, near the end of my semester last month. I was able to drive home and see him since we had a week off from school to prepare for all of our finals. To make a very long and complicated story kind of short, he was very different when I saw him this visit and his parents (control freaks) basically told me that Carl was only home to see his grandfather and not ME, which is another long story as well, but they somehow managed to brainwash their son into thinking that after all my hours on the road home to see him, that none of his time should be spent with me and that I was allegedly trying to 'take away' their son and all this.

Anyway, that aside, he and I were having problems of our own. I still felt the same way about him, but he tried to blame his feelings on Kosovo and said that when he is overseas he has no understanding of love, emotions or anything else and thought it would be better if we split up and ended this three-year relationship. I was willing to try to fathom where he was coming from, whether this was really the reason or if there were ulterior motives involved, i.e. his parents and such. But, the week ended on a good note in general after I had driven back and forth from Miami four times in three days to complete my finals and see him as well.

There were a lot of mind games involved in this situation and I am left empty-handed once again. Our final goodbye was done on my driveway, since his parents thought it unnecessary for me to go to the airport and of course he obeys their...wishes, so afterwards I thought to myself that if he cannot stand up to his parents now about the way he feels about me, then he probably never will. He is a grown man and for him to let them tell him where I can and cannot be is ridiculous. I do not know if it was all this pressure that made him make his decision or a combination of everything besides, but I can assure you that if you were in my situation you would think of it as a lose-lose situation as well.

So now I am working at the YMCA summer camp here in my hometown, busy as ever, taking summer classes for the fun of it and hanging out with my friends. Carl and I haven't spoken in a month, and I recently received an e-mail from him on (coincidentally) what would have been our three-year anniversary last Wednesday that said basically 'Hey, how are you? I have tried calling for the past three weeks and haven't reached you so I guess that you don't want to talk to me. I will make this short, I want to hear from you ...' and that type of thing. He was accusing me of being the one who was avoiding him, when in all actuality, I haven't received one phone call, e-mail or anything since he left and he is the one that is hard to reach!

Needless to say I wrote him back a brief message and now we are up-to-date with the fact that he has failed to return the e-mail. I don't know where we stand. I still love him more than ever, and I know that no matter how hard I try, I will never be able to understand where he is coming from since I am not there to go through what he has been through. He returns to Germany tomorrow night from Kosovo. It is the end of his second four-month mission, so there is not much I can do really. Maybe we are just going our separate ways, but three months ago, he flew me to Germany because he couldn't live without me. Yes, he says that he doesn't want me to be miserable here without him for so long and everything, but isn't that beside the fact? My belief is that if it is meant to be it will be, no matter how much time passes in between these moments in our lives. Please still keep Carl in your prayers as I do, then just send it on back. I am at a loss for words towards him and even if he did call, I wouldn't really know what to say. I just feel like he ended it so abruptly and without even having time to talk about it. Have a wonderful summer, Dianne, and take care. Love always."

One of the advantages or disadvantages of e-mail is that you can appear or disappear immediately. After this last message, Sheri stopped communicating with me and her e-mail address was cancelled. I can only assume that her relationship with Carl ended and it was just too painful for her to put her thoughts into words. But I do hope that for the time we were in touch with each other she found some comfort in just sharing her thoughts and concerns with me, and that having done that, she was able to see the relationship for what it was and move on with her life.

All military spouses have the same issues. We all have the same problems—taking care of our children, houses, cars, finances and jobs—the list is endless. Husbands who are gone frequently. Most of us don't have the support of extended family around to help when we need it. We have to deal with all issues. Every posting is painful, good friends are left behind, new home, new schools, jobs, dentists, doctors, babysitters, neighbors, all have to be found—again.

However, your life is what you make it, for yourself and for your children. Your attitude is what defines you, your outlook and your perception. Change is good and helps you grow as a person. New friends and new opportunities.

Take a deep breath and enter the next stage in your life. Volunteer at the kids' school. Join one of the many clubs on base. Change careers.

Take responsibility for your life, don't blame the military. Help is available from lots of sources, you only need to look for it. Your life is what YOU make it!

Tell me that I am not alone in this one: I had a miscarriage at four months while my husband was away in BiH (Bosnia and Herzegovina) and they (Homefront) took 48 hours to get in touch with him! 48 hrs! It is REALLY hard being home alone and I know that it is a big shit sandwich that we all have to take a bite out of, but how do all of you cope? Asking for help, being alone, 'getting horny' when the neighbor comes over...all the stuff we all experience. Oh, I can't wait for him to come home. Do I tell him I hate the military?

I am twenty-two and engaged to the most wonderful man. He is currently in Meaford completing battle school. Being a part of the Canadian Armed Forces has been his dream as long as I can remember. We share two young sons together who both swear they are going to follow in his footsteps. I imagine I should get to the point: I am scared of the unknown—what is life going be like for me once we are married? Is there base housing available, do the boys go to regular schools, does moving around really affect children or do they adjust easily to it? My list could go on for days and with Josh still in training he doesn't have the time or ability to answer all my questions. I am terrified of leaving behind my family. I know that the military becomes a second family but my concern is that when people find out I have bipolar disorder will they treat me differently. Will they be harder on Josh because of my differences? Any information you could offer me would be greatly appreciated.

I am just a girlfriend. My military boyfriend is black, we are both 25 years old, but because I still live at home, our relationship is being kept a secret. My parents want me to date my 'own kind.' He will be posted outside of our city by September. I have to make a decision if I should go with him or not. If I go, we are definitely getting married. I think every day that I will lose my parents/family because of his race, friends because of the distance, my job, and every one of my dreams to live in a big house in the city and have my children and my friends' children grow up together; all my dreams are gone if I go. But if I stay, then my dreams are nothing without him.

I hope that maybe someone can help me understand. I do not want to move every couple of years; he could be gone for six months at least at a time and then I am all alone. I have no one else to write to. Maybe you can help me understand what it is like, what you have gone through.

Thank you very much for writing back. We have been going out over 1 1/2 years. We were separated last summer for six months. His mother is so in love with me that she wants me to go with him and get married; if I do not go and in time he meets someone else, she has already told him and myself that she is not welcome in her house, because I am the only daughter-in-law she wants. As for living at home, it is hard to move out on your own. I just finished buying a car and then I hope to save some money and move out. I understand about my parents and that they will be very angry, but I cannot love for my parents. I can come and go when I want at home, but it is still hard. I think that my parents do know that something is up; they hint things to me, but I guess to keep the peace they do not say anything.

I guess I have to live my life for myself. You are very right that I am the only one who can make the decision. I have at least two years to think about it because he will have to go on course for nine months or longer (I cannot go with him), then we have already decided that he will get a house/apartment when he is transferred and get settled, and then I will move. I have also decided not to stress myself too much about it right now. When he first told me I was very sad/stressed/upset/confused. I guess we will wait to see what course he will be sent on and where he will be stationed—that will help in my decision. Who knows, all this stress could tear us apart. I have not been through a lot of him going away, but I have experienced it a little, so I have some understanding. I will keep in touch and again thank you very much.

The only advice I could offer this young lady was to give serious thought to all the issues before she made any decisions. She knew I would listen if she needed to chat more, but I never heard from her again.

Keeping the Romance Alive

One question that I am often asked is "how do you keep the romance alive when you are thousands of miles apart." There are as many answers to this question as there are couples living the military lifestyle. This is a concern for mainly young wives who are more than likely dealing with their first long separation. For everyone else, you more or less learn as you go what works best for you. Trust and communication are so important in any marriage and especially in a military marriage when couples spend so much time apart. With Internet service available today, it's so much easier to communicate, but there is nothing that will replace the letter or card that can be read and re-read during some quiet time.

My boyfriend is leaving overseas for a year and, well, we are dealing with a lot of things.... He hasn't left yet and I am curious as to whether or not you have any ideas on how we can keep the relationship we have and build it stronger as the months, even years, go by?

Here are two stories showing how a "newbie" and a veteran military wife handled the "sparks."

The loneliness she felt a short time into their first separation caused one Navy wife to try and think of how she could convey just how lonely she was to her husband. She found a greeting card that expressed just what she was feeling and included an appropriate note. Then she tucked a pair of her black silk panties inside the card, sealed it with a kiss and sent it off to her husband who was serving on a ship.

Equally lonely, her husband and a large group of crewmates were all anxiously awaiting mail delivery. So anxious was he to read her words that as soon as he received his mail, he opened her card and was immediately and totally surprised when the black silk panties dropped out of it. Of course, this event was witnessed by who knows how many other sailors and it's safe to say that his crewmates reminded him of it frequently.

But something good comes out of every situation and her husband learned that whenever he received mail from his wife, he should hold on to it tightly and find a quiet corner out of view before he opened any envelope.

Ken just called. I made him laugh! There are no words to explain the joy of hearing him laugh. I'll share the story with you that made him laugh because ya gotta know I'm a complete moron! Ken had asked for some nudie pictures of me. Well, after six pregnancies and two 20+ hour labors,

I'm not going down that road at this particular moment. So I dug up the Polaroids we took of each other when we were dating. I scanned them and printed them off on one sheet to send over. Which I did. However, I failed to think about the consequences of leaving these photos on my hard drive. Some of Ken's family members showed up to provide moral support, etc., and they wanted to see recent photos of him. Which I also keep on the hard drive. I'll let you do the math and figure out what his family got an eyeful of. Good thing I was one hot little chick. Playboy eat your heart out and then hide me for about 10 years so that perhaps I can face these people again. What ya gonna do eh?

This is my nephew Mark's fourth tour (he is in the Reserves not the regular force) and for some reason this tour has me 'spooked' more than usual. I think it is because a few weeks ago his girlfriend gave him a surprise birthday/Bosnia send-off bash. It was fabulous because I met his friends from different jobs and friends from his regiment. Really nice, nice people. But as I was sitting around talking with his army friends (some from his regiment, others in the regular force or retired from the regular force), we were laughing and talking, sharing stories about Mark before he arrived and I just got this weird feeling that this was his 'wake.' It took me a while to shake the feeling (another glass of wine helped). I don't want to mention it to him to give him stress or to his girlfriend, but my husband certainly hears me talk about it. Mark called last night (he is leaving today) and I tried not to let my fears creep into the conversation because he would hear it in my voice….

I guess I am mentioning all of this because I was wondering if this kind of creepy fear is common? It is strange because on his other tours I worried about him but this one is different and I can't put my finger on why. Maybe an accumulation of tours? What do you think Dianne? I apologize for asking you this since I know you must be busy with your own life but I don't know who else to ask.

I really felt a need to try and put this lady's fears to rest and when I suggested to her that the tragic events of 9/11 plus the friendly-fire incident in Afghanistan the year before had made everyone a little on edge with the current tours, she admitted she hadn't thought of that. I felt her fears and apprehensions were normal under the circumstances as many in the military community that I had spoken to shared them.

🍁 *I'm new to this lifestyle having only been with my husband now for 3 1/2 years. I have two teenage stepdaughters and I realize it is not easy being a military wife and in a reconstituted family. Right now we are facing a new posting and of course the girls are not interested in moving as they are now both in high school, have good grades, are well settled in. The prospect of having to start over in a new unknown area, new school, new friends etc.—how do I deal with this? I also have to leave my present job, which I like. I've been there for 10 years. How do I handle this? A friend, a military wife, once told me that the military has the highest rate of divorces. Now I understand why she said that and the courage she had to stick with it. I just hope I have her courage and strength like you to stick with it. Thank you for listening to me.*

🍁 *I have two and a half months left of my husband's deployment. Although the longest part is done, I feel like this is never going to end. He's due to go on his JLC* when he gets back. That's another 10 weeks. I've been a military spouse for nine years. When do you get used to being away from the man you love? My problem is that whenever he comes home, I start to feel this resentment for him leaving me. I know that this is his job, but I don't know if I'll ever get used to it.* [*first step of a leadership course for Corporals]

🍁 *My husband is due to leave the military environment soon, for two reasons. One is that he cannot take the lifestyle and politics any more as a member. There is as much disregard for their rights and freedoms as many of us feel there is for us. The other is that he feels that by being away from his family for long periods of time, he cannot control the wedge that is pushed between our family.*

I hope that you all take solace in a website such as this and know that much of our pain comes from the inability to voice (or vent) the concerns that are near and dear to us. In closing, I would like to say that we as spouses need to stand by our partners and understand that at some point in their military careers they become prisoner to their pension. We need to do our part to make the family unit work holistically, and know that what pains us pains them.

Chapter 7

Till Divorce Do Us Part

*All I ever wanted was for you to hear me
when I spoke and to hold me when I cried.*

Living the military lifestyle is not for everyone. Unfortunately, most find this out when it's too late—they've already committed themselves by way of marriage. It doesn't matter if your partner sat down with you before the wedding and explained what your life will most likely be like—dealing with long separations; loneliness; needing the ability to be completely independent and yet giving up some of that independence upon his return to the family. It really doesn't sink in until the first time he's gone. That's when reality kicks in and you find yourself alone with all the family responsibilities, and no one to depend on except yourself.

Many thrive in the military atmosphere, but for some this lifestyle demands too much. For others, they have started to ask the question: "Is this life really worth it?" Certainly with today's world uncertainties, the added stress, worry, and fear of the unknown have taken their toll on some spouses. Living sometimes thousands of miles from the support network of family and relatives, some spouses just can't handle the heavy load.

At the same time, the military man is dealing with all the same emotions. His frequent long absences from his home often make it difficult for him to fit back in. While I have heard from many women who are dealing with divorces, I know from my experience that many, many men are also dealing with the sad fact that they just can't be everything their wives need. But just like any other group, some marriages don't last for 101 reasons not related to the demands of the military lifestyle.

My husband held a long and protracted affair with a [woman who was in a] common-law relationship. Together they managed to ruin two families, resulting in the death of one member, and finally destroyed my oldest son. Here's to the two of them—may they reap what they have sown. Two more selfish, self-centered people you could not meet, and they deserve each other.

The following story was sent to me as a result of the author viewing my website. I felt her opinion was just as valid as any other and so I contacted her to let her know that contrary to what she expected, she had a right to her opinion, even though not many would share her viewpoint, and I would most definitely post her comments on-line. I felt she just needed to vent and that was OK. Obviously she was not coming from a happy place in her life.

I am sorry that I can't share your joy in that web page. I am actually looking for a page for women who were married to military members—like I was. In fact, my divorce is not even final yet. I was quite surprised how little support there is for women who get divorced from a soldier. I was married 12 years to a member of the Air Force. His job and career always came first. I went through one war and one crisis (Bosnia) with him. But was there support? NO! You always had to have a smile on and pretend everything was fine, so how can you say the Canadian Forces are the best? As soon as you leave the member, you are on your own. The military washes their hands of you and if you are lucky enough you get stuck in an isolated posting. He gets transferred, but I should sit here? I didn't ask to come here, it was my Ex's job and the kids and I went too. He gets all the support he needs and for me, it's a struggle. But I'm glad I am out of this life. I have one good thing going for me. I'm strong and have willpower, I have a good lawyer, friends who are in the forces, and I will get through this. Our soldiers don't have a good reputation anymore, that was a long time ago. From what I gathered, you are an Army wife. I've seen stuff in the Air Force, it is unbelievable. But like it always was, don't let civilians know anything about it. Pretend. Young girls should know before they sign on the dotted line, what they are in for. I considered myself a good wife; I always supported him, stayed by his side, and never complained. Raised the children 75 percent myself. I didn't hang out in the clubs or anything like that, but I got my reward for it. Divorce. And now I am fighting for my rights. And one more thing, if the Canadian Forces has the highest divorce rate, now why is that if there is so much support? I've seen a lot of friends breaking up. You probably won't like my message too much but somebody has to come out with reality. —Anonymous

Her comments brought a flood of responses:

I honestly find your letter disturbing for two reasons. The first one being the fact that you think the military owes you something because you were married to a military member for 12 years and you are now going through a divorce. The second is that you don't seem to realize that you are the only one in control of your life. There isn't a company in the world that provides support for spouses after a divorce. In fact, most of them don't provide support for couples during the marriage in the form of marriage counseling. At least the CF provides that for couples.

You are the only person in the world that can make you happy. Our life is filled with choices and we are the only ones that pay the consequences for our decisions. One of your choices was to get married to someone in the military before you were self-reliant enough to make it on your own and now you are paying the consequences. You wrote, "Young girls should know, before they sign on the dotted line, what they are in for." Maybe that is the problem. Maybe too many young girls are getting married before they have a chance to become self-sufficient women. If you don't have the confidence to be alone and independent before you get married, how are you ever going to have it after you get divorced?

The best thing we can teach our daughters is self-reliance. Educate them, praise them and let them know that they are capable individuals. Give them the skills to cope alone in this world. Give them their own support system.

I have just finished reading Anonymous' letter. I feel really bad that your experiences with the military have not been pleasant. I am about to turn 40 this year and have been with the military all my life—first as a 'dependant daughter' and then as a 'dependant wife' and I can honestly say that except for a couple of minor hurdles, my experiences have all been wonderful. When my children were old enough to understand, I told them to treat each move as an adventure and I think in a lot of ways that helped us cope.

My husband is in a combat unit and has been gone more than he has been at home (at least that's what it feels like sometimes). [These times gave us] the opportunity to draw closer together as a family. We have been through tours to Europe and a year-long tour to Bosnia. There were some tears and upset but that's when we had the support of neighbors and friends, and as well there was support from other sources to help us through. I don't think I would change too much of the past 40 years. Take care, Anonymous, and I hope you find some peace and comfort.

I have to agree with the Anonymous poster. When my husband and I separated in our second year of marriage, I was told to call the Padre as things were really getting out of hand. I called the Padre and was told that he was there to counsel marriages that were still together and not ones that had already fallen apart. Can you believe it? Luckily, we were able to work on our marriage without the help of the military. I don't know what I would have done without my fellow military wives and their spouses for their help at that time. The military didn't want anything to do with me or my son at all. I gave up a full-time medical career to follow him and raise a family. We have had good times and bad times but I really feel that when you do a marriage preparation course like we did at the Base, it should include more information on what it's REALLY like to be a military spouse.

I have carefully read the letter from Anonymous a few times. Then I read some of the responses. I am a military wife of 10 years whose husband has just spent the last six and a half months in Bosnia (certainly not his first long stint away from home). During this time I have made the choice to leave my job to stay home and be supportive to my children (my position had involved shift work). I continue to bring up two small children who ask every day where their Daddy is, and I am limited in the ability to get out and do 'personal' stuff. I deal with all the household issues, school issues, three sets of stitches that my children have acquired, and all the day-to-day tasks that face me every morning. There are days when I am resentful and certainly feel sorry for myself, but I can't imagine that being in Bosnia/Kosovo is better than being around my children, family and friends. Having the ability to eat a Big Mac, go to the beach, take a walk in the woods, have coffee at Tim Hortons and eat Sunday dinner with our relatives is a gift. I also took this time to take night courses at university and take cardio-kickboxing two times a week. No one gave me this time, I made it!

I have seen many military friends have their marriages torn apart and was very saddened by this. I have also seen others become stronger and closer. I have also witnessed non-military friends go through divorce and others make it through tough times, only to become closer. Certainly being married to people in the military has its stresses, but so does being the wife of a police officer, truck driver, businessman, doctor, lawyer…and the list goes on and on. It is easy to blame the military for our personal and marital problems. That sometimes gives people an out instead of looking at themselves, their personal happiness and self-reliance. It also keeps them from taking a good look at their marriage and the problems that exist. It is nice to receive support from the military when my husband is away, but the support I receive from HIM both at home and while [he is] away is what helps us get through these times. I do empathize with Anonymous. It is very difficult to be married to someone in the military. It certainly is not for everyone and it does not make you a weaker person if it is not for you. However, it is also not fair to criticize the entire military for failed marriages. There are many of us who have had our husbands away and we continue to survive these separations. People and their choices/support make or break their marriages, not their jobs. I also want to take the time to thank the people at NDHQ [National Defence Headquarters] for their support while my husband is in Bosnia.

I too have read and re-read Anonymous' letter and the responses. I don't think it fair to blame the military for failed marriages. It's the couples who make or break their own marriages. I was in the military myself and got out to raise our family. Three months after our first baby, my husband started sailing and [went on a] NATO [tour]; 11 months later he was home. One month after our second baby was born he went overseas. As I write this now, he is gone on another NATO tour and will come home in four months' time. Trust and communication are two of the best ways to help keep things going smoothly. I don't have a lot of family support, I always hear, 'You made your bed, now lie in it' but I have my husband who doesn't want to be gone any more than I want him gone. We've been married nine years and to Anonymous, face your own problems—the military isn't it—and move on. The Military Family Resource Centre has a lot of support things going on—call them!

And from two gentlemen readers:

I have been part of the military for over 25 years and I have numerous peacekeeping tours under my belt as well as exercises, etc. I came into this Regimental family when Family Resource Centres were unheard of. My advice is look after your needs; if you are emotionally happy, independent and self-sufficient, you will learn to cope, to deal with the ups and downs of this world. At times you may not think that there is help out there. It's there, but you also have to help yourself first. We have more support systems in place than any civilian company can offer—just use them. To Anonymous, good luck in your new life and I hope that you will some day look back and find some good memories of your life in the forces.

I'm not in the military and never have been. I came upon your web page quite by chance and must congratulate you on this unique and most valuable concept. It has provided me with a view of military life that I otherwise would not have had. On a personal note, I feel that the Anonymous writer of the letter who expressed her dissatisfaction with how she was treated by the military after her divorce was treated rather shabbily herself by some of the respondents here. She bared her soul and was told in essence by some people that she had nothing to complain about. The callousness of some of the remarks was surprising!

In response to my e-mail to her, Anonymous, who now seemed in a better frame of mind, responded:

Thank you for your response. I was actually surprised to get a response. I would like to take you up on your offer and e-mail with you. Thank you very much for that. Please understand that I am not against the Forces; it is their policies, and as you may agree, some of the members in the Forces shouldn't be in there. I am a mother of four and my oldest son is going be a fighter pilot. At the moment he is on course in Borden so I don't think it would be good if I condemned the Forces altogether. I do support my son in every decision he makes for his life, and that's his life-long dream to become a fighter pilot so he has my full support.

… Maybe I was too blunt, but please do understand the position I am in. I

have to fight this battle all on my own. All my family is overseas. I know I will make it—I am a fighter. But sometimes it gets very frustrating. I am a Canadian citizen and love Canada. I mean, I could write a book here, the way I was living with my Ex who is very controlling; even to this day he is trying, but it would be too long. But I did learn quite a lot while I was a dependant. For one thing, how to do things on your own. During my marriage I lived on Air bases, and it is different. But anyway, I really did appreciate your response and would like to hear from you again.

Not only did she and I correspond regularly for the rest of that year, but she did identify herself to me, sent me a picture of her and her four children and let me know when she was able to leave the restricted northern posting her ex-husband had brought her to (with the help of a social worker). The last I heard from her, she had a new partner—another military man.

· · ·

One of the saddest messages I received was an open letter to an ex-husband, which appeared in my website guest book. The depth to which this lady bared her soul reconfirmed to me just how much of a need there is for women in this challenging lifestyle to reach out and connect. Not just with anyone but, more importantly, with their peers. They are the ones who truly do understand.

To my now ex-husband from your now ex-wife:
All I ever wanted was for you to hear me when I spoke and to hold me when I cried. All I ever wanted was for you to understand that just because I don't leave the house to go to a job, it didn't mean that I didn't work. It didn't mean that I was never tired, never stressed out, and never needed a break. All I ever wanted was to go places and see things with YOU. We never made it to New York or Maine or Prince Edward Island. We never even made it around Quebec City.
You know everyone is so much into 'Steven-bashing' and it bothers me. They don't even know you. They don't know that there is a good person somewhere in there. But I know. I know he's there, because I've seen him. He's the man I fell in love with. And he's the man who'll always be in my heart. Whether or not you want to accept it, we will always be connected to one another. We

have a bond stronger than anything now. We have our baby. But, the man I leave in Quebec today is not my Steven. I don't know where my Steven went to, but he disappeared from my sight a long time ago.

My Steven was sensitive and caring and loving.... My Steven wasn't afraid to hold me when I was feeling down, or to sit with me and talk for hours if need be. He would take me out to places even if going out for just a drive was all we could afford. He cared about the things I was interested in even if he didn't fully understand. My Steven promised me that if I gave him the chance, he would prove to be the best husband and the best father. He promised to fight all those who would hurt me; he promised to always be there for me; he promised to make all my dreams come true....

I don't know where 'my Steven' went to; all I know is that he never came back. I tried to love the man who replaced him as deeply, but it wasn't the same. The man who came in place of my Steven is cold and uncaring. This man could not hold me. This man had selective hearing and would tune out all that he didn't want to hear. This man didn't care that someday I would love to be able to write well enough to be published. This man would tell me to do something with my life and then get upset with me when I tried. This man broke all of those promises and in turn, broke my heart as well.

This man brought our family to an unkind, uncaring province and alienated me. He left me alone all the time to deal with how I was feeling and what I was going through when all I ever wanted was to be able to lean on him; to cry when I needed to cry; to be held when I needed to be held; to be heard when I needed to speak.... And of all people to understand how difficult that transition was going to be was my Steven. He went through the very same thing when he moved to his first posting all alone with no family and no support network. And this man never seemed to understand that I didn't need anyone else but him. He's all I ever needed....

At one time, Steven, I really did love you with all my heart. I remember telling you that I love you more than there are stars in the night sky. It wasn't a lie, Steven. It was very much the truth. I would have done anything for you. I already left almost all that mattered to me behind to move with you to Quebec and keep our family together. And all that I ever asked for in return was to have your support, to have your understanding.

I hope you will be able to believe me, someday, when I say that I tried. No matter how many times I was ready to give up on you, I stayed. I spent the last two years fighting with myself to stick around. Some people said no matter how I felt, I should stay. I should stay not for me, not for you, but for our child. Others were telling me to leave because it wasn't healthy for our baby to be stuck in the middle of an unhappy couple.

I tried; I tried so many times to tell you how unhappy I was. And now that our family is destroyed, don't ever think that I am happy now because I am not. I never wanted it this way; I never wanted this to happen. I kept telling myself that if I stayed, things would get better between you and me. I kept telling myself that if I could just get you to hear me, then we would be able to work through all of our differences.

I accept the fact that you are in the military and have chosen to serve this country as your career choice. I understand how stressful it can be. Don't forget I was once a part of that too. I understand that there are times when you couldn't always be at home with 'my girl' and me. The times when we were apart were tough but we made it through them and could have continued to do so. But after all that I have been through in trying to find my baby and get her back, I will never trust you or the military again. You lied and they covered up those lies for you and justified your actions to be those of a sane and competent father. And as strange as this may sound, some day I will be able to forgive you. The pain that you caused our dear little baby to endure will come back to you. And you won't find mockery or ridicule coming from me. You will find only a deep sense of pity. Pity, Steven, because things didn't have to turn out this way. All you had to do was come home and talk. All you had to do was to say that you weren't happy in the relationship we shared and that you wanted out. Despite all the legal costs the agreement we came to was done out of court finally, so it could have been all settled without having to get the legal system involved at all. Pity because you will then and only then have some understanding of the pain that 'my girl' is going through now and went through when she was taken away.

I feel hurt that we couldn't make our love last the way we had wanted to. And I feel anger because of your rash decisions and [misguided] train of thought. It will take some time to get over all of this and be able to move on with my new life as a single parent. But I accept that we are BOTH at fault for the downfall of our relationship. I don't know—maybe what I expected from a husband was too much.

Take care of yourself. Always remember that Sarah loves you. And so do I— just in a very different way now, but love nonetheless. —Ann

This next story was another sad tale of a marriage that did not survive the overwhelming demands of this lifestyle—but I didn't find that out until after the exchange of a few e-mails. The Navy man had contacted me through my website's guest book and I was so touched by the poem he sent that I contacted him. As part of his submission to me, he had included his wife's e-mail address, requesting that anyone that read the poem and liked it let his wife know. His comments from before he sent the poem I found to be very valid and so I'm sharing them with you here:

I have spent the last 10 years at sea with the US Navy. As many of you know, sometimes we military men (not just sailors) will bring our work and frustrations home with us. You are left to deal with the family, the bills, the homes, and to top it off, your husband. Well, I too am guilty of this and it has taken its toll. My wife is finding it hard to believe how much I appreciate all her sacrifice for our country and me. I have been trying to express to my wife that while I was away, she was always first in my heart.

I did contact his wife because I thought the poem would touch hearts but I was surprised to receive a reply from her asking that I remove the poem from my website. It appears that she and her husband had separated two years before and the poem was a desperate attempt on his part to make amends. It was too little way too late. Of course I honored her request, as she was not impressed with having her e-mail address published in such a way. I felt such sadness for them both as she and I exchanged messages. It was obviously a situation in which a husband didn't know what he had until he no longer had it. I couldn't help but wonder what part the long absences from home played in this marital breakup. We'll never know.

As I have often said, no matter what country our partners serve, military spouses are universal in that we all go through the same emotions in this lifestyle. This sad, sad story is just another example of the difficulties of keeping a marriage alive and well in the military community. Sometimes the obstacles are just too great to overcome.

This next military wife's story had me really concerned for her well-being and stability and I immediately felt such compassion for her that I wished I could have given her a big hug. There are just so many ladies dealing with such uncertainty in their relationships and while I know this isn't just restricted to those in the military lifestyle, it is sometimes much harder for us to deal with. How can you work on your problems when you are so far apart physically for such long periods of time? How can *you* be trusting and loving and accept the fact that your partner isn't?

July 10

Hello. I was wondering if there was anyone else out there who finds themselves a wreck? My husband is in Kosovo and I am having a hard time dealing with this. It's the first time this has happened. I just need someone to talk to. I read the poems on your website and started to cry. This is so hard for me. Any ideas? Just e-mail me!

This was the first time I felt a need to speak with one of my correspondents. She just sounded so desperate. However, my request for a phone number to contact her was answered with *Hi. I would like to continue to talk to you but would rather not give out my number. I would really be interested in what you have to say! Thanks.* When I thought about it, that was the right response for her to give. She didn't know me at all and it isn't wise to just give your phone number because someone on the Internet asks for it. My compassion for her situation overshadowed my common sense in asking for her phone number. And so our e-mail exchanges began and I did my best to "listen" when she felt like sharing. We exchanged some small talk about the weather and job-hunting and for a while the conversations involved just generally learning more about each other.

July 13

I got a letter from my husband this last Saturday. He says it's really sad over there and he is very busy. I swear I am married to GI Joe!

July 16

Well hi again! I've been sort of busy and not very social lately. My sister-in-law, who lives a couple hours away from me, opened a letter that was addressed to my husband. The mail sometimes goes to his Dad's house because that is where he used to live and he got in trouble with the law while he was down visiting his family. I was here with my folks and he had our car and was pretty intoxicated and well, you know the rest! So, the court is sending paperwork to his Dad's home and his older sister took it upon herself to open the letter and then called the courthouse to find out information. Well, I am mad because it is none of her business and his Dad should have just sent the letter to me because I wrote to the courthouse to ask some questions concerning his case. I am worried that he will get in even more trouble because he is not taking any ADAPCP (Alcohol and Drug Abuse Prevention and Control Program) classes, and that was the deal. So, do you think I have a right to be upset? I am a pretty sensitive person. But, to me there is no respect there. His sister has been like a Mom to my husband and they talk all the time and we never discuss what the conversations are about. I guess I feel like I am in competition with her. She also asked me when I received his letter and said she was going to send him care packages, which I think is a nice gesture. I'm just not too close to his family I guess. They are too nosey for my taste. I feel like I am growing apart from my husband every day and it just kills me. Well, today is not so good as you can tell! Write me back sometime and tell me what you think!

July 23

Sorry I have been out of touch for a while. I guess I haven't been very talkative. Well, I am over the 'sister' thing. I told my husband and we dealt with it. I finally got a letter from him yesterday and he called me this morning at 2:30 a.m.! It was good to hear his voice. He is having a real hard time, I think. It's easy playing a soldier but being one is a different story. I think he is facing that reality the hard way. He now is running his own Colt/Cav [combat observation and laser] team that has a couple of guys on it. He's just been so busy and has little time for himself.

Correspondence with Sarah dwindled, as we both were busy with our own lives. However, I did send her a message after Christmas that year asking how she was and letting her know I was thinking of her.

February 8

Well, things are slowly looking up. I have been just a wreck these days. My husband came home from Kosovo the first of December and then he came here to spend Christmas with me and to see his family also. We had a wonderful reunion and it was so nice to see him. It was very weird at first, but things seemed to settle in okay.

Her husband was posted from his Kosovo tour directly to Germany.

He left again, having been here a month.... I had two jobs that I quit because we both figured I would be following him back to Germany.... Not so. 'They' lost my paperwork three times and then had sent it back because they needed a copy of our marriage certificate (which is in Alaska in our household items). So, I had to call around and finally got hold of someone to send me a copy so I could then fax it to my husband....

I finally had enough and so has my family seeing me go through this terrible situation...so I e-mailed the LTC [Lieutenant Commander] of the Battalion a very nice letter explaining my situation and so on. Well he mailed me back saying he was very sorry and that he informed the BC (Battery Commander) and 1st Sgt of my husband's battalion. So, my husband calls me the next day and says he read my letter and not to be sorry. I think he was impressed that I stood up for myself. And he didn't get into trouble.

So now my husband has left for PLDC [Primary Leadership Development Course] to make his E4 [rank – pay level enlisted] and won't be back until March 10. So, I am trying very hard to find another job and have to explain my situation to my employer but won't mention that I will hopefully (keeping fingers crossed) be leaving in March.... I really want to get my life started. I have been waiting 11 months—almost a year.

I have been diagnosed with clinical depression. After he left to go back, I had a complete breakdown. I am now on medication that is helping a little, but have a lot of things I need to address in my life through therapy or something.... Now he tells me that he wants to go Special Forces. I don't know how to feel about that. It will be interesting to see if he goes through with it. I think he is going to try. He says he's not going anywhere in field artillery... go figure....

Well I hope all is well with you Dianne. Sorry to pour my heart out to you. I am just having a hard time coping...hope to hear from you soon.

By now I had a strong suspicion that the "system" didn't lose her paperwork that many times. It can't process paperwork it doesn't receive and I wondered how long it would take her to realize that, after 11 months, her husband just didn't want her to be in Germany with him. Of course, I couldn't broach that subject—it wasn't my place to do so. But I agonized over her waiting and waiting, giving up a good job and an apartment to move back in with her parents while waiting for the day she would be joining her husband.... It just wasn't fair!

I am not doing well. I told you that my husband came back here for Christmas. Well, when he was here I thought that everything was pretty much okay between us. As things turned out, when he returned to Germany he didn't call me for a week or so. I didn't have a number where I could reach him...so I finally called around Germany and got hold of him. After I got hold of him he was shocked, I think. He said he had just been busy going to work and he was supposed to be getting my paperwork done but he wasn't trying very hard.

Then I got a call from one of the wives I met in Alaska and she called and asked me what the heck was going on with our relationship. I had no idea what she was talking about so the next day she had her husband call me and tell me that my husband [had called him when he] was very drunk and had said that he was having thoughts of not being married and he didn't think he wanted me to come to Germany. Well, I was heartbroken. So I asked my husband about this and he never remembered calling him and saying those things. But before this he had e-mailed me and said that he wasn't going to lie, and that it is easier being on his own. See, he is living with the single soldiers and he has always pretty much been on his own and our marriage is tough!

So, while he was at school I went down to Oregon to see my very best friend from high school. What a blast we had! She wants me to move back down there and say goodbye to my husband. I didn't call my husband for a week and he was really worried about me and he asked me if I met anyone else. I love him and he is the only one I have known in a relationship so it's very hard to [objectively] see things that he does or I do to him. It's hard for me to think he has been faithful the whole time.

My paperwork has been lost over there five times. I have e-mailed the LTC over there twice and it seems that only one of the pieces of paper always just disappears. This time they say my husband didn't turn in my EFMP [Exceptional Family Member Program] paper we would need to get housing. We had to go all the way to Ft Lewis to get this…piece of paper—[it's] gone, no one knows why, so I have the LTC working on it.

I won't be there to put on my husband's E5 [rank – pay level entitled] pin after his graduation. He said the school is a joke. He says he's tired of being away from me and that he loves me so much and I have nothing to worry about. I feel like he likes [having] me home by myself waiting for him. My life is on hold. I don't have a job because I thought I was leaving. My husband comes back March 9, so I am hoping I get over there after that, but I don't seem to have any hope left in me…. Write me back please and tell me what you think….

When telling or reading a story, true-life or not, everyone likes a happy ending. However, I don't know how this story ends because Sarah's e-mail address was disconnected. That didn't end my concern for her or her well-being, but it taught me that this is sometimes the way of e-mail communications. Exchanges can be made only until one or the other can't or won't continue. I could guess the outcome of Sarah's story but I will never know for sure. Perhaps, this was just another example of reaching out for a connection, only to sever it when it became too painful.

I wonder if any other military spouse had her husband grabbed by an ex-military wife. It amazes me that one woman could willingly take part in an affair while she knows the wife knows nothing, and then get engaged to this man before he is even divorced, come to the base where the wife lives and go to his retirement dinner in the wife's place—needless to say, I am insulted. Hurt! I would have never been part of anything so low. I was a good military wife—always home working downstairs, knitting while an ex-wife was taking my husband over the Internet!

The hurt and pain many suffer in unhappy relationships can be difficult to read about and difficult to write about. But it is nothing compared to what those involved in the dissolution of their marriage must feel. While I have recorded only one side of the stories in this chapter, I felt each person's comments were important to share, including the following tale of how the long separations and accompanying stress can deal the final blow to those who aren't prepared, or can't handle this long time apart.

My name is Jackie and we are currently residing in Alberta. My husband returned from duty in Bosnia in 2000. He was gone for almost seven months and his unit only called me once in the entire time that he was gone. Things were very difficult for me and I had very little support while he was gone. The stress was enormous for both him and me. On his return to Canada he immediately asked me for a separation. I guess the stress got to him and he hooked up with a female military officer in Bosnia. However, I digress. My children and I have survived almost a year now without any support from the military, whether it be when he was away overseas or when he returned and asked for a separation. I am a slightly bitter, almost ex-military wife who gave 14 years to the military and received absolutely nothing from them in return.

Today, many young families are looking at their troubled marriages and are deciding not to continue in them, even for the "sake of the children." Whether this is a good thing or a bad thing depends on whom you are talking to. I wanted to include some comments here from military wives during the 1960s, as their mindset was considerably different from that of today. Only you can decide which is the right path to follow.

My mother told me when I married my husband, 'Don't come home; come home to visit. Don't come home and tell me Jake's doing this or Jake's doing that or I don't like this and I don't like that. I don't want to hear it. You marry who you marry and you make your bed and that is where you lie.' All three of us girls (sisters) were told the same thing, and all three of us girls are still with our original husbands.

Today, if John does this and Mary doesn't like it, she says, 'to hell with you' and she's out the door and vice versa. Or, if she does something that John doesn't like or doesn't keep the house the way he wants it kept, or supper is not on the table, he then says, 'I'll find someone else who'll make it for me.'

I was brought up to believe when you choose a man you choose him for life so if you don't like the way he behaves, don't marry him in the first place. You have to really know the person before you marry him. And I knew my husband.

I knew he was a drinker. He wasn't a drinker to the point we were left alone all the time, but to me, it was a lot of drinking because I was a non-drinker. My Dad wasn't a non-drinker, he'd have a few beers on Saturday and that was the extent of it.

I guess there were times when I might have said, 'I'm going to walk' but then I thought about the way I was brought up and my mother telling me, 'You don't do that. You have children. They need a structured life.' I guess I learned that I could put up....

I was married in the '60s when military life was so different. In fact, my ex-husband ruled the roost and I had no idea what was going on—with his job, the military itself, how much money he earned, etc. I think nowadays people are more open and communicative with each other (at least I hope they are and don't end up as casualties like I did).

The young man's story that follows is a very sad one and shows clearly that, sometimes, love just isn't enough. Since his military trade was a highly specialized one, I've taken great pains to tell his story without including comments that might identify him. I owe him that for his complete willingness to share what he did.

I joined the Navy at a very early age. Everything was great....
Challenges, proving myself, [being] surrounded by extraordinary men, doing extraordinary things. Except that there was no softness in our lives, no beauty, no women. None. None. None. So, after six years, I left to go to college, mainly to find love. I found her my first day of class. Or more accurately, she found me. Six years later we were still together and I asked her to marry me. She said yes. But I still had to earn a living so I rejoined the Navy and went to sea for two years. I could hardly wait to be on the bridge and see the stars and work on intense missions. I loved it and she said that she would wait for me. I believed her. She believed herself. Despite my passionate pleading, the two years was extended to two and a half years, and then to three years. Five weeks before I was to finally leave the ship, and seven weeks before our wedding date, she left me. I can't blame her—it was too long. What to do? After [this was] a short stint in a land assignment; ironically I was now just five miles away from her office and home, instead of 3000 miles, and I still never saw her.

I volunteered for another sea assignment. There was no reason to be on land. I sailed to remote regions and worked the ship for about a year, getting my mind and heart healed. I came back to a different land assignment and started to get my life in order. I did. I was taking evening classes to get certified as a teacher, and I was painting all the time. I was happy.

And then I met a remarkable woman. We fell in love, got a house, and I spent the better part of two years building a life for us. In my off-duty time, we built a paint-your-own pottery studio for her with the money that I saved from being at sea. It has been a great success mainly because she is an amazing artist, and exudes joy to everyone that is around her. After seven years, I resigned from the Navy to live a happy, normal life.

However, the bills came and came. I still had to earn a living. I tried to get any land job that I could, but my skills just did not transfer over to the civilian world that easily. To avoid losing it all, I took a job with a private sector firm. I was always told that you [could] make loads more cash in the private sector, and have a life too. Well, I have been doing that for a year…and I make less than I did when I was in uniform, a lot less. And I am still on ships and never home. Our marriage is sorely strained.

I am on the brink of both bankruptcy and divorce. Something has to change. So I just put in my two weeks' notice. What to do now? Strangely, the Navy wants me back. I guess that they are having a hard time finding and keeping highly qualified people who are willing to go to sea for two years at a stretch. They can find social misfits who want to run away from life. But they don't have the skills to run complex high-tech missions. And they can find men who do have the skills, but these men are very rarely social misfits, except for those like me who are on the edge of being a social misfit.

Anyway, the Admiral (another remarkable woman) is reviewing my files and will be sending me a letter in two weeks to be reappointed to the Corps. If I sign it, I will be in uniform again and immediately assigned to a ship. Six more years, get command of a ship, and then retire, probably as a full Commander. Solves all of our financial worries. But leaves our hearts longing and unfulfilled. I don't think that I can be a good officer anymore, now that I know what it means to love someone. But part of being a husband is being a good provider. I don't know how this will turn out. And the sex issue is pivotal. Part of wearing a uniform (if you are a nice guy) is to ignore your own sexual needs for long periods of time. You harden yourself to it. You really have no choice. I am just now realizing how much damage this has done over my adult life…just as much damage as if I were a scoundrel and womanizer. And as important as this issue is to me, it is even more important to her. She is a woman, a beautiful woman, and she feels that she was made, both physically and spiritually, to live an intensely passionate life with a man whom she loves.

Ralph and I continued to correspond while he waited for the Admiral's letter. It's impossible to give advice when you learn only one side of the problem, and so all I could offer was a listening ear and a place to vent, as long as he felt safe in sharing. I tried to be encouraging and sympathetic where I could, but how do you help someone when you feel their heart is breaking? When they appear to have done the best they can to make a happy life for themselves and it's just not happening?

I am still waiting for the Admiral's letter—it could come any day now. The 'different generation' aspect is perhaps the most important issue when looking at how my situation impacts society as a whole. If it were just one naval officer facing this issue, it would be no big deal for our society. But my experience is that most of today's naval officers will face the very real threat of divorce during one of their sea tours during their career. Times have changed. Expectations have changed, particularly women's expectations. Today's officers are simply responding to those changed expectations. All officers who cannot meet those expectations will pay a very high price. Unfortunately, prolonged absences while at sea simply do not fit in with the expectations of most of today's women and the price is often divorce.

If the price of being a naval officer becomes too high, then men will stop being naval officers. Of course, it is a matter of numbers. Maybe in past generations, the effects of an isolated divorce here and there did not put a strain on the Navy, but how do the Navy and the Country deal with it when divorce becomes the norm, and officers routinely cut short their careers to save their marriages?

Through all of this, I have to stress that I find no fault with wives not wanting to put up with the hardships of a military marriage. The expectations have changed, but that does not mean that the new ones are necessarily wrong.

About two weeks later I received another e-mail from Ralph and I expected to read some good news. I had so hoped that he and his wife had been able to try to make their marriage work "one more time" despite the challenges they faced to put so much hurt behind them. However, I was saddened to read Ralph's words which were the last I was to receive from him. I can only hope that once he gets his life in order, he'll contact me again. But, I suspect that he will work hard to put his past behind him and that includes sharing so much with me.

Things do not always work out as planned Dianne, or as hoped for. I got accepted back into the service, but I failed the physical. My cholesterol is too high. I have the option to be re-evaluated in 90 days to see if the medication has brought the numbers to acceptable levels. But I'm not going to try. In the meantime, my wife could no longer wait and admitted to having an affair. We are getting divorced. She is getting the house. The ironic thing is that within a few days after all of this went down, I got an offer for a pretty good office job. I start in 11 days. Until I get my first paycheck, I have $200 in my wallet and will live in my truck. There may be a lesson in all of this but I can't see it right now. I am just getting through the day a minute at a time.

Actually, I can think of one lesson—I will never go to sea again. It's time to let someone else answer the call. I have a life to start living.

Chapter 8

In My Opinion

Your life is what YOU make it.

One of the most popular pages on my website is the "In My Opinion" page, where different topics are posted and people can comment on them anonymously. Their identity is known to me but is not posted on the website. The length of time a topic stays on-line is determined by the responses to it, and some really good e-mail conversations have emerged over the years. This following response was part of a discussion on the lifestyle in general, and I thought her comments really spoke for many.

Hi. My hubby was in the USN [United States Navy] for 11 years. I don't think you can truly know what you're getting into until you're there. The thing is, it's a tough life but there are rewards (you just don't see them at the time). For example, my hubby teases me about what a quick learner I am. If the sink leaks I climb under and fix it. I can pay the bills and figure out how to get by on very little. I have two children with him. I've seen places and met people I never would have. Those are benefits. They are thanks to the Navy life.

Oh sure, the memories are not all great, but I learned how to get along with folks who aren't so easy to get along with. I have stood eye to eye with his captain and sized him up while he did the same to me. I learned how not to back down and when to back down. The big thing is—Do you love your man? If you let God help you, you can get through [anything]. (I can do all things through Him who strengthens me.)

I came across a leader of the wives' group, who lectured me about not to

158

expect my hubby's presence just because I might lose our baby or die myself (problem pregnancy), when all I had asked was that he be notified. I figured he had a right to know. We got into it but the thing is she was half right. I never would have asked my hubby to come home—it would always be up to him—but I needed to always be self-reliant and never expect him to be there. I was married to him but the Government owned him and he was always going to be required to answer to them first.

He wanted to volunteer to go to the Gulf during the war. I may not have liked it but I would support anything he wanted to do.

Love does not boast, is not jealous, it is supportive and kind [Corinthians 13: 4–5]. I always knew who he was coming home to. I was proud of him and our life together and lived for that time. I kept a journal/letter telling all, sent pictures, made some videos. There were always homecomings to look forward to (and plan big time for). Our first years out were pretty wild. It was like being newlyweds because we spent so little time together that we were truly getting to know one another. That was actually a worse time than the loneliness. We went from things going the way I was accustomed to, to having to let him in.

An article in the *Toronto Globe and Mail* (September 20, 1999) focused on a military family in which the husband and wife were each required to go on a tour to Bosnia at approximately the same time, leaving their 10-year-old daughter behind. Many who read the article, which is too long to be repeated here, found the reporter to be prejudiced against the military, and to lack understanding of the obligations of military personnel. The article contained a number of questionable statements. I posted the full text on my website's "In My Opinion" page and the response was fast and rather furious. Excerpts from the article are shown below, as well as several of the responses. You can form your own opinions.

MS [Master Seaman] Jones had recently returned from a two-year stint in Croatia when his wife Cpl [Corporal] Jones, a truck driver, was told she would be going to Bosnia. Days later he learned that he, too, would be going. Both then tried to get out of the tasking but each was told it was a job requirement.

Then the rounds of meetings with support workers started as they tried unsuccessfully to have at least one parent remain behind, as they had not made any arrangements for care of their daughter. She was finally sent to live with her birth father.

'We were all crying. We always told her that we would never, ever go away together. And then it happened. It was very hard. She would call my mother-in-law every night and say that she was worried that we wouldn't return, that we would both come home dead. We felt the military made us abandon her.' MS Jones said.

So traumatized by having to leave her daughter, Cpl Jones never called her daughter—not once in the whole time she was away. 'It was too hard. I was numb. I was in Bosnia. I had a job to do.' However, MS Jones called his daughter every day.

Because of advice they received from a support worker that they felt was totally inappropriate, they complained loudly on their return to Canada, which resulted in apologies from DND left, right, and center.

'Ten months is like forever when your child is not around. The turmoil from this lingers,' said MS Jones. 'My daughter didn't sign on the dotted line to serve her country, and she's the one who suffered the most.'

My response (on my website) to this article was as follows:

While I fully realize that reporting can be difficult if you don't understand the nature of the item you are reporting on, I also found this article (if you can believe what is in print) to show the couple in question, a medical technician and a trucker, to be users of the system, and they came across as wanting their 15 minutes of fame to last a lifetime.

When you draw a salary for a particular job, you are expected to perform the requirements of that job. As long as you are accepting the paycheck, you can't pick and chose what aspects of the job you will do and not do. The fact that both husband and wife were in the military was THEIR CHOICE. They were wrong to promise their daughter they would never go away at the same time.

When push came to shove, the Cpl had a choice to make—her job or her daughter. It's obvious that her job came first—otherwise she would have taken her release and remained with her daughter. Too harsh a statement? I don't think so. Military wives quit their jobs all the time to follow their husbands and their husbands' careers—this is no different.

The fact that she was 'so traumatized' she couldn't talk to her daughter in

the 10 months she was away is unbelievable! Give me a break. That's a very selfish attitude and shows that she was only thinking of herself—not her daughter.

When both parents are in the military, they are morally obligated to have a contingency plan in place when children are involved, in case they have to be away from home at the same time, whether it's on a course or tasking. To turn a blind eye to the possibility of this happening was irresponsible on their part. To wait until it happened and then run from pillar to post whining to get out of a job requirement is also irresponsible. No blame can be put on the military, as far as I am concerned. This couple wanted to have their cake and eat it too—at their daughter's expense. They, and only they, are responsible for this whole sad situation.

This article upset many in the military community for a variety of reasons. It just goes to show how quickly people can jump at the written word, whether it's true or not. Is this story true? Possibly. Are the facts correct? Not likely. Did the reporter do his homework? No—that was obvious. Articles like this one attack the very core of our military community, and we don't deserve it!

I just read your comments on the situation described in the newspaper article regarding the parents who were required to be away at the same time and forced to leave their child behind. I can't imagine any organization with an awareness of the importance of parental presence in a child's formative years removing both parents from the child's life in the name of duty. I find that bewildering.

I read this story in the paper as well. I was quite surprised by it. I too wondered why the couple did not have a plan in place for when something like this might happen. I also wondered if the story was correct. I was under the understanding that when soldiers return from a tour they must remain at their home base for six months before being sent on another tour. I too believe the parents are at fault here. If I were the mother, I would have quit my job to stay home with my child.

To say that a parent can't go on a six-month tasking because his or her partner is going, and there would be no one to look after the

children, would be the same as saying every single parent in the military does not have to go because they do not have a partner to look after their children. Stop blaming the system for what is a parent's responsibility.

I find it very hard to believe that the military would not have insisted that they have some kind of plan for caring for their daughter. It is understood that if you are in the military, you will be going away. Even married members (whose spouses are not military) are encouraged to have some kind of plan in place in case of emergency. I think they were kidding themselves if they actually thought they would not be sent away at the same time.

My only comment is that it doesn't always have to be the female who quits her job to care for the children. The father in this case had the choice to do the same thing.

I too find fault with the parents. They should have had a plan in place. When I was pregnant with my first child I was in the military and my husband was leaving on a seven-month NATO tour and I was posted, so I got out to look after our daughter. That's not saying everyone should do that, but as I said before, you must have a plan.

I find the article to be unbelievable. I cannot imagine the military forcing the father to go back right away [after he had] been there originally for two years. I haven't ever heard of a married father stuck in Bosnia for two years, considering both of their trades and the fact that there are so many people that want to go. I also find it unbelievable that the military would force the parents to leave their only child alone for 10 months. Sounds like another reporter that wants to paint ALL of the military, from the top brass to the soldier, with a bad brush. This reporter should have been called up on the carpet for this one.

I agree with the fact that the story this couple has relayed to this reporter is a boldfaced lie. The time periods of these deployments (2 years and 10 months) are very odd and given the new quality of life initiatives, this scenario is highly unlikely in the context outlined.

I was rather disturbed by your suggestion that the woman quit her job to stay home with the child, specifically because her husband had just returned.

Why should she not have the opportunity of an overseas tour? The child is 10 years old and should be independent enough to sustain six months without her mother even though separation is always difficult. I find it hard for any mother to believe that she couldn't call her daughter because it was too difficult. Boo Hoo! They need to take their whining to someone who cares...if they can find someone.

When you have completed a tour outside of Canada you will not be tasked for another tour unless you sign a waiver giving the military permission to task you for another tour. So, if the father signed a waiver I guess the father should look up the definition of sympathy, as it clearly does not apply in this situation. I'm curious—did either parent return to Canada on their mandatory UN leave to see their daughter?

I too find it hard to believe that one tour would be placed so closely after another. However, being a wife of a military member who has served on three six-month tours, I was always left behind as 'rear party' to perform the duties of both mother and father to my two young children, duties which ALWAYS took priority in my routine; any jobs I had took a back seat. Where are the maternal instincts in both these parents, especially the mother who couldn't even pick up a phone to comfort her own daughter? Shame on her. Tell me really, who's the adult and who's the child here?

I just read your article about the 'family' that had to leave their daughter behind. A lot of it makes no sense at all. When our spouses go on a tour we all have to sit down with the padre and/or social worker. They ask us about how we feel and if we can manage, how the children will cope. There would have been ample opportunities for either parent to have made a 'stink' about going. They chose not to. A 10-month tour—I don't think so—especially not for both. I know a number of families that have both spouses in the military and if they were to object to going away at the same time there would have been different arrangements made. I think this is a case where the parents were selfish in the respect that they didn't want to turn down a tour because it may look bad for their career. Not calling your child once, because she was traumatized, yeah right! I won't even go there because I find that totally irresponsible. The father, on the other hand, I give credit to. When my husband was in Bosnia in 1997 he was able to call every night. I was very fortunate to have that. I agree that our children didn't sign on the dotted line, the parents did, but you have to know where that line is drawn, especially when it comes to the family. We all have back-up plans as to where our children will go if 'something' should happen, they should have had, too. I feel this article had a lot of holes in it that were either not researched properly or The Jones family forgot to mention. This is a perfect example of how one shouldn't always believe what is printed. The only person in this 'story' that suffered was the child!

Regarding the military couple with the daughter—as a fellow human being, mother and military member, I am rather disappointed to see so many negative and highly judgmental responses. Regardless of this family's circumstances and decision, right or wrong, we are often fed a one-sided view from the media...so why did so many respond with only the facts that the media provided? Time to switch to another topic that will instigate more thought-provoking discussion. I suggest 'Has the quality of life for CF families improved, subsequent to the SCONDVA hearings?'

• • •

The purpose of the discussion page on my website is to promote dialogue on issues that are of interest to many. I was so pleased to see this site used by the guys as well as the gals:

I am a military husband and I can relate to everything mentioned on this site. I am facing a two-year sea assignment during which I will see my wife only 30 days a year. Six more years to retirement and the loneliness and separation is just not worth it anymore. I want to break the cycle and live a normal life together. She craves a full-time, loving husband, someone who sleeps by her side and holds her every night. (It seems that nobody honestly addresses how important sex is to a wife that feels neglected and untouched for two years.) And now that I know the warmth of a genuine hug, I value that above all else too. However, financial difficulties of dropping a 14-year military career will bring new types of burdens to our marriage. A question to the wives on this site: If your husband came home and said, 'I have to choose between the security of my career or a life of love. I choose love. It will be scary, because I have no idea how to make a living outside of the uniform.' How would you deal with this?

My first thought is, I would hope that my husband would never come home and just say, 'I'm quitting my job.' It would be very scary to think of just leaving this lifestyle without another job waiting and I would like to have been a part of that kind of decision. If this is what he really wanted then I would support him. I have faith that with 14 years of experience, finding a new job would not be that difficult. The fear of the unknown is natural but I'm sure that, with both partners willing to do what needs to be done, you can overcome this hurdle and have a great new life outside the military. I guess it comes down to that I would rather have him doing a job that makes him happy than one that puts more strain on our family.

Oh my word, a difficult decision! My heart goes out to him and his wife and what they must go through! Hubby made a choice between the army and me. I had made it clear I could handle the absences, etc., but he couldn't. He missed me terribly and it really bothered him that he was missing the most important years of our son's life. I think the final clincher was when he had to sit over the Autobahn in a watchtower during the Gulf War.... It really came home to him then. It was scary, the remuster, and hard. His CO [commanding officer] was not pleased with his decision to go Air Force, but Kevin insisted, and he's not looked back since. As to getting out, he's scared out of his wits about it. He doesn't like to sit down and talk about it, and has left the planning up to me, which makes me uncomfortable. He's hanging on— they do need his skills and personality for the type of work that he does, it's not as simple as people think. However, he will have to face a decision at some point, and I'm dreading that day, because I know his decision will not be an objective one. I think that gentleman in the Navy is a very brave soul for what he is thinking of doing, and kudos to him for it. Not everyone can cut it with the length of time away, and he's wise to realize it NOW instead of at SEA.

I have had a few moments to pause, and collect my thoughts regarding a response to the military husband. The way I always look at sit-

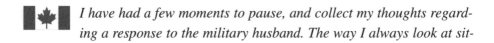

uations such as his (life-changing decisions) is to ask myself if, at the end of my life, I would have regrets about not following my heart at that fork in the road. While I recognize and understand that money and financial stability help make life easier, they do not, in my opinion, bring about happiness. I have a couple of friends who have just recently had to make the same decision. From what they have shared with my husband and me, the decision to leave the military lifestyle was not an easy one. However, since making the decision, they have not had one regret. I would be totally supportive of choosing love over lifestyle. You only have one shot at a lifetime together—be sure not to have any regrets in the end.

Chapter 9

Medical Issues

You left our father over there—go bring him back!

One of the biggest stressors for military families today is the scarcity of doctors available to treat new patients. Although this is a national problem for civilian families as well, it's one of the biggest concerns for military families—especially if they have a family member with special needs. Military wives have always felt that two of the biggest problems with any move are finding a new doctor and finding a good babysitter—both essential parts of this lifestyle. But the severe shortage of doctors today is a major concern and is definitely a factor to be considered by the family when they are facing another move. Many families don't want to give up their current physician to move to an area where they may be placed on a year-long waiting list for a new one. Even healthy families are worried about what will happen if they suddenly need a doctor.

The only reason I got in with a doctor in Edmonton is because friends of ours had been posted to Kingston and I was able to talk the doctor's office into letting me take their place. They had two kids as well. I had phoned around and it was definitely an issue. As for having a special-needs child, it is out of the ordinary, and care across the country is anything but standard. Like I mentioned, he was on a two-year waiting list in Edmonton and we moved before he got therapy of any sort. Here in Ottawa, it has been different with regards to special needs. As for a family doctor, I phoned every office in Orleans and only one was taking new patients. Then of course you get the new person, or the doctor no one wants. I feel my family's care has been good—though if I had a choice I wouldn't choose him.

There are walk-in clinics, in many locations, that can be used for emergencies or minor ailments but they do not provide continuity of care.

I went to the walk-in clinic and the doctors there won't fill my prescriptions from my psychiatrist so I don't know what I'm going to do. I wrote to my psychiatrist (at my last posting) to ask him if he could help me but I haven't heard back from him yet. The doctor who wouldn't renew my prescriptions told me that I could call the hospital and get a psychiatric evaluation to figure out why I have to take medication, but not to stop them because it wouldn't be good for my health. So I wish someone could please tell me what is going to happen to me. Luckily, I have two refills left, so it buys me some time.

I'm just not too keen on the military right now. [They] put me in this godforsaken place and forget about me. I have a long road ahead of me if I'm going to go off my pills. I was not the one who prescribed them for me in the first place and I wish someone would take responsibility for this.

It wasn't that many years ago when families were asking why the military doctors couldn't expand their area of responsibility to include the families. It made sense to many of us. But it never did happen and today there aren't enough military doctors to look after military members. On some bases, civilian doctors have been called in to help lessen the workload of the military doctors so that our service members can have adequate medical treatment.

Recent initiatives to attract more doctors to the military were unsuccessful. Unless a doctor has a strong desire to live the military lifestyle, why would he accept lower pay to work in the military community and also be expected to serve in wartorn countries? Most are looking forward to working in an environment that offers more than the military can.

To address this shortage of medical support for our military families, some military bases are attempting to entice doctors to come to their base by establishing a family clinic on the base and furnishing it. Many families hope that in due course the majority of bases will be able to establish a similar system. But if the local civilian community has a shortage of doctors to look after their needs, where are we going to find doctors to look after us?

[For] military families to be offered fair, good doctors in their own community, who understand the lifestyle, would be beyond helpful—it would be amazing.

Many military wives have experienced going to civilian doctors who don't understand our lifestyle and who paint us all with the same brush. They say we're paranoid, suffering from imaginary illnesses, and they don't respect us the way they should. While not all doctors fit into this category, I was amazed at the number of wives who told me they had seen doctors who treated them as if their illness "was all in my head." Or said that "I was just looking for a little attention because my husband is away a lot." It appears that Canadian military wives aren't the only ones who must deal with this mindset:

Our doctors think that military wives are a bit of a pain and over-dramatic. We are not. We just have a lot to put up with. One of my friends here has just given birth, her father has died and her husband is off to Iraq soon. The doctor told her she is a bit overdramatic. He put her on Prozac!

Adding to the growing list of worries that today's military families must face—more tours, more danger, more apprehension and worry—is the stress of not being able to find proper medical care. One can only hope that a long-term solution will be found to help military families who desperately need one.

Post-Traumatic Stress Disorder (PTSD)

One of the biggest concerns facing our military families today is post-traumatic stress disorder. It is only one of several conditions that military members are suffering from but it appears to be the one that is causing the most concern. As one military wife said to me, *Please explain PTSD to me so that I can understand it.* According to the DND website, *Post-traumatic stress disorder is a psychological injury caused by the reaction of the brain to a very severe psychological stress such as feeling one's life is threatened.* A professional explained it to me this way: *A critical incident is a traumatic event that goes beyond our capabilities to cope. It is a psychological wound. Post-traumatic stress refers to the symptoms one may develop after a critical incident, such as increased heart rate, nightmares, flashbacks, thoughts of suicide, etc. Post-traumatic stress disorder results when a person cannot cope and the symptoms persist over a period of time causing problems in a person's ability to function.*

Certainly, with the increase in NATO tours for our military members and the requirement for so many of our troops to go on repeated tours, the incidence of PTSD seems to be on the rise. There is no doubt in my mind that those service members who are required to go on multiple tours are at greater risk. How can you face danger day in, day out and not have it affect you in some way? As one soldier put it: *The longer you are away the more you have changed.*

Another soldier expressed his concern in a way that I'm sure echoes many others' sentiments: *My biggest fear? Is the bullet going to miss the flak jacket and hit flesh? What is a big issue with the wives at home is not a big deal here when we are worried about our next breath!*

When I first decided that I needed to acknowledge PTSD in this book, I wasn't sure what I could include. Not having any medical background, I felt I couldn't really get into this complex issue, but since it is so prevalent in our military community today, not to acknowledge this condition would be doing our families a disservice. And so, I asked, as part of my research, what support DND was providing military wives to help them help their partners who might be suffering from PTSD. The responses I received to this question were unanimous: *Nothing!* In fact, it looks like DND is just now getting a handle on treating service members suspected of having PTSD.

Unfortunately, at the beginning of our struggles with this up-and-coming disorder (around 1996), DND and members affiliated with it put up huge barriers in assisting us with recognition, support and treatment. Since this has become a chronic disorder now my husband has been given a medical retirement (which actually has been more of a 'you're not normal—here's the door'). SISIP [Service Income Security Insurance Plan] is providing him with a college diploma in Architecture Technology and he has had to separate himself from us to go into the world and try and find himself again. It is both a relief and heartbreak to have him go. Our three children have been on the roller coaster with us (actually my husband has been on his own roller coaster).

My oldest son, who is 13, has truly been put to the test. He is an amazing young man and is a veteran of his own accord. My younger two just don't really understand why things are so crazy. Veterans Affairs has been our main support. They have a lot to learn as well but they have connected us with the support systems we presently are connected with. My husband now sees a civilian psychologist who specializes in police and military trauma. She has a very active practice in our small military population here. This office has connected my children and me with psychologists of our own, which has been crucial.

This is a family disease and it is very dangerous and painful. As well, the office has organized a spousal support group which started out well-attended but has dropped off lately. We are a fairly diverse group of women from 20 to 80 years of age, at different levels of living with and dealing (or not dealing) with the disorder in our lives. We did, however, share a lot of common ground with dealing with many of the same kinds of issues with our husbands and with the military. There is much bitterness towards the treatment our guys received for their problems. I have kept in contact with a couple of the more mature ladies in the group and this has been a huge support. The groups were very draining and I think it was maybe more than some of the women (no guy spouses in this group) were willing to endure at this time.

It's common knowledge in the military community that most men feel it isn't macho to show your feelings or to admit there are things bothering you. So peer support just isn't there as it should be with those suffering from PTSD. Co-workers tend not to believe there is anything wrong, and resent carrying a larger workload because one of their own isn't "pulling his weight."

I have found in my research that there is a definite stigma (in the military community) attached to having PTSD. *One wife contacted the MFRC asking for help in dealing with her six-year-old's reaction to her husband's PTSD. 'Oh, your husband is one of those kind of guys,' was the reaction she received to her request.*

Those that suffer from this condition are reluctant to admit they have it—for a number of reasons. Fear that admitting they need help will place them on the stressful road to being released from the Canadian Forces often causes members to try and "tough it out alone." In a recent TV interview, André Marin, the CF Ombudsman, stated that it is a "given" that those who suffer from PTSD will eventually be released from the CF. When you have spent your whole adult life in the military community, have a family to support, and are not well, the fear of being tossed aside while you are ill and perhaps unable to adequately look after your family adds considerable stress to an already stressful illness. *'The guys don't trust the system so they won't confide in it.'*

Many feel they need to be treated for their illness outside the military circle. They need to be free to seek civilian help. They also seem to have the attitude that "you weren't there so you couldn't possibly know what I'm going through" that shuts their wives and family out. Their peers don't believe them but feel they are just trying to worm their way into an "easy medical pension."

However, a Peer Support Counseling program instituted by DND in the last two years is one step towards providing a listening ear to those who are willing to seek help. One criterion for becoming a PTSD counselor is that you yourself must have suffered from the condition. It is hoped that by talking to someone who has experienced PTSD, military members will open up—for their own good.

The importance of education in understanding and dealing with PTSD cannot be stressed strongly enough. Peers, families and support centres need to know exactly what this condition is before they can deal with it.

DND must also find a way to offer support to the families of those suffering from PTSD—not 10 years from now, but NOW! The mindset that we have to treat only the military member just isn't going to wash. This illness affects the whole family. The system wants the whole family's support of its members—especially during tours—so it stands to reason that the system must support the family when that support is most needed—during the illness of a military member.

In an attempt to understand this issue a little better, and to find out how other groups of individuals dealt with severe stress, I interviewed some paramedics. One of the main differences between paramedics and military members is that paramedics are encouraged to talk with their peers about traumatic events and discuss what's bothering them, while soldiers are taught to separate themselves from their emotions. And while military members deal with the horrors of war for six months at a time, paramedics deal with death and dying every day—there is no let-up for them, it is an ongoing aspect of their career.

One incident that was particularly difficult for one paramedic to deal with was the suicide of a childhood friend who had been a member of his wedding party. He had killed his wife before taking his own life, leaving their child alive in her crib in another room. It's one thing to deal with the loss of life but when you know the individual personally, it can be extremely hard to leave your emotions behind.

A paramedic had to respond to an emergency call from his own home where he found his parents attending to his six-month-old son who had a high fever and was convulsing. I can only begin to imagine the emotional state this compassionate man was in as he realized he was rushing to his son's side—not knowing what he would find when he got there. The emotional strain of working in a small community where everyone knows everyone can be great. It can be difficult to handle unless you learn to get a grip on your emotions (and let your training take over) to keep you from identifying too closely with the person who needs your help.

One paramedic said that the only emotional support he had received was at an accident scene where a 13-year-old girl lost her life. He had a daughter the same age. His supervisor asked him if he wanted a drive home…. He further stated that there is no special training; you are just left on your own to deal with whatever comes your way.

The atrocities seen by our troops are of a different nature—the deliberate taking of lives, sometimes on a large scale as compared to accidental death and suicides—from those seen by paramedics. Paramedics seem to be able to vent their feelings with their peers while military members tend to keep it all inside compounding their problems. *Communication is so important to a paramedic, being able to 'talk it out' and not keep it all bottled up inside—that's how you survive in this lifestyle.*

If talking it out is the solution for paramedics, what's the solution for military members?

The following, compelling story left me crying on the inside for the family involved. But at the same time, I marveled at the daughter's courage and willingness to share such a heart-breaking family story as seen through her eyes. I hope all who read this story will offer a silent prayer for a family that has had to deal with far too much, and for a man of God who is really in need of those prayers.

Dad joined Navy when he was 16 and got out at 22. He got married, and rejoined the Air Force as a Padre. In 1993, he went to Rwanda. We were used to him being gone in Halifax on ship so it wasn't too much of an adjustment except the added stress of knowing that he was in a HOT country, with the firing and whatever. My sister and I were at a friend's place on New Year's Eve and he called us to wish us a Happy New Year. When I spoke to him I heard machine-gun fire and it sounded like it was ricocheting. Then we didn't hear from him for a week. It was awful. I was 16, my sister was 14. My sister had a harder time with Dad away. She went through the extremes of rebellion as you can imagine.

When he came home, he was definitely different. We used to make jokes, 'You left our father over there—go bring him back,' not realizing there was actually something wrong. But all he could talk about all the time was Africa. He used to send home pictures and videos and things for the archives here, and Mom would hang on to them, and not realizing what they were necessarily, my sister and I would watch them. They were pretty gruesome. Just video footage of fields and fields of dead people everywhere—pictures of bodies and things. He actually wasn't taking the videos, someone was taking them and he was just in charge of sending them back.

Being 16–17, not even realizing—so that's what he does, you know? Who does the padre go to when he needs help? And it got worse. He started getting very angry at everything. Bad mood all the time, short-tempered, depressed, and didn't like doing things, acting very strangely—doing things he wouldn't normally do. Picking arguments over nothing in particular. And, I guess, things were happening that we didn't necessarily know about. He was having nightmares, dreams, flashbacks. We noticed his memory was awful—couldn't remember a thing. Like, you could tell him something and then he'd ask you—you'd have to tell him again and then he'd ask you, and it was strange. He seemed to think it had something to do with Mefloquin but who knows? Then one day I got a phone call. I had gotten married and moved out and got a phone call to say that Dad was in the hospital. He had been walking into a chapel here on the base. There was a bit of a hill up to the door from where you park. All of a sudden he stopped and they saw him rolling down the hill. They went out to see if he had fallen—he was tucking and rolling from sniper fire—he was hallucinating. So they took him off to the hospital and from that point to his actual release (from the military) was close to three years.

When he was a padre [in Rwanda] he had to deal with all the children in the orphanages and that sort of thing. He had one little guardian called Tony. He picked up enough French to talk to him and he had grown close to this little guy. He dealt with all these orphaned children. There was one little baby that they didn't think was going to make it and he named her Star. He fought to have her brought back here—couldn't do it with all the rules and things they have over there. He wanted to bring her home and adopt her back here but he couldn't do it.

I think dealing with death in such a horrible manner on such a large scale is bad enough, let alone all the children. He talked about Africa all the time but he never opened up with us about any of the experiences that bothered him. His therapist suggested he put some of it in writing, which would just get things on paper so he could let them go. He did write one article for the Legion magazine and I read it and it said things that even I didn't know. My mother said she didn't know them either. It said in that story that, because he was the padre, whenever they would come across a church—for whatever reason these people felt they needed to slaughter churches full of people—he would have to go in and remove the sacrament from the altar.

They went in to do this at one particular church. He was removing the sacrament and they heard a movement. They didn't know if it was an animal or something but they thought perhaps someone had survived so they started taking the people away and searching for what it was. What he found was a mother who had been shot holding her baby, and the baby was alive, but it had been days. He picked up the baby and she died. And, I mean, something like that here, let alone in the middle of that, is enough to make somebody require some help. And it was just thing after thing after thing like that. When he was over there, he had a buddy, George. I think he might have been his driver. It was Christmas Eve, they had just had their little service, they had their two drinks or whatever, and everyone was in a pretty good mood going back to their room. Dad heard a gunshot; he ran next door—George had shot himself. He had to call George's family Christmas morning and tell them. My Dad is really the kind of person who refers to them as his guys—his kids. He really takes on, from my point of view, maybe more than he has to, but I'm sure they love it.

They ended up putting him on sort of like restricted duties sending him up to NDMC (National Defence Medical Centre) with the lawyer and the Sergeant Major of the regiment—they stuck really close—all being released together. They went up and had to do their interviews, and evaluations and tests and whatnot. Then they'd come home and have to go back and eventually it got to be that everyday stresses just got to be too much. People were finding out that this was going on and they all thought that he was either crazy, faking it, or trying to get out.

I'm sure you know PTSD has a pretty bad reputation—it's the easy way out. You're the weak one, buck up, you can take it. The padre? He's used to this stuff—he's faking it, he just wants to get out. Eventually, he was put on a medical holding list, and sent home. He had to go to the base once a month kind of thing and then he ended up that he couldn't go to the base at all. Just going to the base was bad. He has a therapist in town now and he still sees him regularly, probably once a month. In the summers he's taken to biking—he bikes everywhere, all the time—that's how he relieves his stress.

He ended up being released last year. I would have thought he would be relieved after fighting so long with SISIP and medical and having to get the documents for this and that and the other thing, that he would be relieved that it was finally over, seeing that he hadn't been to work for two years anyway. But it really depressed him to have to accept the idea that he was no longer in the military.

He can't even go back to the church as a civilian. You never know what is going to set him off. He is on medication. He was on Zoloft, but after they put the bunch of them on Zoloft, something like seven of them killed themselves. So they took them off Zoloft. Of course this isn't well-known but when you lived on base and associated with these people [you heard about it]. He is on medication and now he is dealing with a civilian doctor.

I think the saddest part for me to see: growing up if it was a snowy day, and we were going to miss church, we had church at home. That was him—church was it. He totally lost his faith all together—in the church, religion, that kind of thing—and for Dad that was just not where I saw him being at this point at all. He was so involved. At one point, there he was, thinking about going back to the church and everything, and then he just walked out all together and didn't want anything to do with it. Wouldn't go to church anymore. Got rid of all his vestments and things.

Now he bikes and plays on the computer. He finds that he can't come back to the base—he tries his best to avoid situations where he might run into someone who might know him—because he doesn't want to talk about it. He goes to Remembrance Day parade—every year he puts on his blue beret and every year someone comes up to him as asks him something or says something to him and he comes back and says, 'I'm just not doing it any more.' But every year he goes back—he can't let go. I think he wants so badly to remain part of it all.

I think he has been so discouraged by previous treatment that he wants absolutely nothing to do with any support programs that DND or the CF has to offer. He just doesn't want to deal with them. From doctors telling him, 'buck up and get over it,' from the military social worker saying, 'he's making it up.' Never once did anyone ever call my mother to see if she was all right. As for his peers, other than the odd call to see if he left something in his office, no they didn't call—at least not that I am aware of.

I met my husband through our unit. He was actually a reservist at the time as well. When we got married, I never really thought about it until he was going overseas. All of a sudden I started having all these thoughts: what if he comes back like Dad? What if something happens over there and he comes back like Dad? What am I going to do? I found myself searching websites daily and newspapers and things. Bosnia is a nothing tour now—not much going on over there. I found myself searching the newspapers and stuff to make sure nothing happened. Every time they found a mass grave or someone had stepped on a mine or something over there I panicked that he was near it or saw it and was going to come back a different person. It took me until he came home at Christmas and was pretty much the same guy to ease up on my worrying a bit. But when he came home he was a bit different—luckily for the better, I think anyway. I find that after he has been away, the little things don't bug him anymore.

As for things that happened at home while he was away, he always said he wanted to know about them because he didn't want to find out about them later. I didn't want to tell him because I didn't think he needed any more stress than he already had over there. So, you know, I had a car accident, someone drove into my car, I had oral surgery, and kids were sick, little things like that. I have a harassment complaint against my boss, and that started while he was away. But I was trying to cope with that stuff and trying to make it seem like it was no big deal.

I know he could go to Bosnia and come back fine and walk across the street and get hit by a bus, but the idea of it happening so far away is what gets me. Not having seen him much before [he left] and the possibility of never seeing him again is what scares me.

Chapter 10

Permanent Married Quarters
(PMQs)

What's wrong with this picture?
The 860-square-foot PMQ I lived in 45 years ago in
Winnipeg is now renting for $700. The mortgage on my
new 2600-square-foot home in Winnipeg is $640.

On most Canadian military bases, a number of housing units are available to be rented by military families. The units vary from apartments and row houses to duplexes and single-family homes. For military families who have to adjust to the nomadic aspects of the military lifestyle, it has always been a comfort to apply for housing at a new destination and have it waiting for them when they arrive. The fear of the unknown can cause a great deal of stress in any military posting; knowing that you will have a place to live once you get to a new area, where you might not know anyone, can be a big stress reliever.

I can remember when military families were discouraged from living off-base. Military members were expected to live as close to bases as they could, to ensure that any call-out of troops could be accomplished as quickly as possible; the way to do that was to live in PMQs.

I can also remember when a group of our friends decided that they wanted to try and put down some roots. We were all posted to Gagetown at the time, and most in this group were Maritimers. And so, with building costs relatively inexpensive in the 1970s, these friends, who all had different skills, formed a co-op and vowed they would help each other build homes. Much time and energy was spent on researching the intricacies of a co-op as well as on shopping for the best and most reasonably priced supplies.

The group had reached the point where they were just about ready to start building, when posting season rolled around. Although they all knew that postings were part of the lifestyle, many saw this new home as a place that they could rent out when they got posted out, and that would be there waiting for them when they returned. At the time, there were only three main posting choices for engineers, and so the chances of their returning to Gagetown at some point were fairly good as the engineers were all early on in their careers.

At this time, CFB Valcartier, a Francophone base, was expanding, and so the engineer family was to expand there as well. Many felt it wasn't a coincidence that most of the co-op executive were posted to Valcartier, even though many couldn't speak French. And so the whole co-op crumbled with so many being posted out at the same time. We all took this as a warning to stop considering living outside the base. However, if that was the intended outcome, it didn't work. More families, fed up with sub-standard housing and little, if any, repairs, opted to find other accommodations.

It wasn't long before you could drive around the PMQ area and see unit after unit—empty. DND wasn't hesitant about collecting the PMQ rents, but they weren't putting the money back into maintaining the units. People were just fed up with "fighting" for repairs. They didn't feel they were getting their money's worth in PMQ accommodations and so they started finding other places to live.

To try and regain some of those lost funds, DND was offering PMQs to RCMP personnel, and then to civil servants working on the base. DND still had plans for the rental income they had come to depend on and so it was common knowledge within the military community that as soon as the troops received a raise, the PMQ rent would go up! It always looked good in the newspaper headlines to read that the government was looking after our troops and families and paying them more, but you never saw the fine print showing that while they were giving with one hand, they were taking back with the other.

Somewhere along the way, DND stated that the PMQ rents had to equal civilian rental costs in the same area so that they weren't taking rental opportunities away from the civilian landlords. We all just shook our heads in disbelief. We live in a unique lifestyle, and having access to PMQ living was and is considered one of the trade-offs of this lifestyle.

Skip to 30 years later and today you'll find that many PMQs have been torn down and many more sit empty. Why? Because the rate of deterioration has continued just as the rate of rental increases has skyrocketed. The justification? One base commander told me that the PMQ rates are high because you are paying for the privilege of living close to your work area! Garbage! They are still trying to milk military families dry.

How can military members get to and from work when they live off base? Not only will civilian rents increase when they have no competition from PMQs, but having to travel a longer distance to work also increases the cost [of getting to work]—higher [car] insurance, higher fuel costs, more wear and tear on the vehicle. Not to mention that if both partners are working, living off-base will mean the extra expense for many of having to purchase a second car. It's just not fair!

Most think the reason for high rents is to justify the mindset, "Well, people aren't living in them anymore so we might as well tear them down because we can't afford to heat them." They are trying to justify their desire to rid themselves of all PMQs.

[DND's reasoning:] *We can no longer subsidize [homes for] a group of military personnel. We are helping them to build up equity by purchasing their own homes.* Well, not everyone can afford to buy their own home, particularly today when it takes both parents working just to maintain a reasonable standard of living. Nor does everyone want to own his or her own home. My response to this shocking statement was to say that if you want people to settle into the civilian community and buy their own homes, then you have to tremendously increase the length of postings. Why should military families feel forced into buying a home when they know that a few years down the road they will have to move? Can the government guarantee that they won't lose money on their home when it comes time to sell? I don't think so.

Granted many families are choosing to go this route and "take their chances" and many more are settling into their own home and not moving when their husbands are posted away. Either way you look at it, DND is once again not giving enough consideration or thought to the military family. When we no longer have PMQs, we will no longer have a military community.

When you consider that all PMQs will likely be gone by 2020 (torn down or sold), you also have to wonder what the MFRCs' role will be when we no longer have PMQs. Since the majority of those making use of the programs the MFRCs have to offer are the residents of the PMQs, who is going to use the MFRCs when the PMQs are all gone and the military community is no more? I posed this question to the commander of a base on which PMQs are currently being torn down. His response: *Then the MFRCs will have to work harder at their outreach programs.* I don't think that's going to work. For families spread out beyond the base, traveling to the base for the services of the MFRCs will no longer be convenient.

Two-income families already say they are too busy, between work and home, to have time to use our MFRCs. What is going to change in the family dynamics to increase attendance at our MFRCs? The distance families will have to travel to access the MFRCs also has to be considered, especially in an era where time is already scarce, expecting more attendance at the MFRCs is unrealistic. On one hand, DND says it can't justify subsidizing housing for a group of military families by providing PMQs, but isn't it already giving subsidies to a group of military families through the MFRCs?

Just to give you an idea of how families feel about military housing, I've included a few responses here, which show the good, the bad, and the ugly aspects of the situation.

I loved growing up in PMQs—such a feeling of community. I'm now married to a serving member, and we don't live in them. The PMQs were old when I was growing up. A sub-standard, non-upgraded PMQ is not a deal, as far as rent goes anymore. Of course, there are still areas that are an exception to this, but on the whole we've found a mortgage cheaper, and the home comes with new windows and an attached garage. Would I rather live in the PMQ community? In a heartbeat. The loss of the PMQ family life is tragic, especially in light of the elevated [number of] deployments.

There is nothing that can replace neighbours who know exactly what you are going through when your spouse is away. Now the rents are so outrageous most people would rather have a mortgage (if you have the down payment). The PMQs in Toronto are so bad that the windows are rotting out. The rents for new tenants this posting season are $1,200 to $1,300 a month; even with PLD [Public Liability Damage] (which has gone down again) it is not worth it. Quality of Life (QOL) is obviously not important for the families here in Toronto.

My first experience in PMQs was in Baden Baden as a child. It was fun, sharing life with kids who were in the same lifestyle as my own—especially living in a foreign country. Years later, I married a military man and found myself with my own family living in PMQs in Comox. With his being a private at the time, it was a godsend to have the Qs. I live in PMQs now in Shearwater and love it. To lose the PMQs would be terrible and would create such problems for many families who can't afford some of the outrageous rents in town or the even-harder-to-get mortgage. I can see postings becoming nightmares if the PMQs are let go.

I will do basic upkeep on my PMQ—that's not a problem. I can fix a toilet flapper with duct tape if I can't get to self-help! The stuff that bugs me is the lowest bidder thing. I have seen half-assed jobs so many times it is sad! When someone thinks it is a good idea to change the back door on a PMQ and leave an empty space there for over an HOUR when I have two kids to try to keep warm in FEBRUARY, something is decidedly wrong. Also during that same job they didn't have a door handle for me. I just had a dead bolt for a week and a bit. Housing informed me that it was fine—no one could fit his or her hand into the hole, etc. What about my kids' hands or someone wanting in bad enough they could use something else to get the dead bolt undone? But, just think on this—my Mom's first PMQ was a converted chicken coop! How's that for creativity?

And here we go again with the pay raise and then the rent hike. How is it that this happens every time? By the time the rent increase comes out and the taxes come out, I think we make less than before the raise. But what really bothers me is that the media reports these raises but never reports that our rent and taxes go up, so the civilian world thinks we make all this money. Oh well, such is the life that we have chosen. Maybe one day we'll get that raise and be able to put it towards something we might need or better still, something we might like to have. Thanks for listening.

When we moved into the PMQ that we currently reside in, records showed that nothing—absolutely nothing—had been changed or updated in the PMQ (floors, bathroom, carpeting, counter tops, etc.) for at least 20 years. And they chose not to refinish our floors, change the linoleum

182

or do various other jobs so that they could get us into the PMQ faster (thus to bring in the rent again). We have been fortunate that through diplomacy and [perseverance] we have been [able to get] a new counter top, bathroom (the old one was unhealthy and unfit for people to use) and new carpet on the stairs since we began to reside here.

Having lived in a PMQ for years, you must have been witness to the contractors that did the repairs and upgrades. We had windows put into our house last year. Not once did any of them use a level while installing the new ones. And on more than one occasion we 'caught' the contractors trying to cover up a mistake they had made but didn't want to take the time to fix. Let us not even mention the condition they left our home in 'while in construction.' The inspector was disgusted when he saw the mud, snow, dirt, gouges, etc., throughout our home. Perhaps these homes would be in better repair and in need of fewer repairs and upgrades if in the first place they hired contractors who cared about the job they did—and didn't get it because they were the lowest bidder!

 Damn shame! I feel safe [now] letting my kids play outside—that comforting feeling will disappear with the PMQs!

According to the minutes of the Military Family National Advisory Board meeting of June 2, 2002, which appear on their website (http://www.mfnab. forces.gc.ca/engraph/home_e.asp)**:**

***Canadian Forces Housing Authorities (CFHA) Presentation** – Ms. Roszell, CEO CFHA, gave an update on the future of Married Quarters and CFHA's intention, with appropriate approvals, to reduce MQs to approx. 9,000 and to get out of the MQ business in urban areas. Ms. Kelly pointed out that these housing decisions had significant impact on members on Imposed Restriction (IR) and single members. Ms. Dunn commented that by 'getting out of the MQ business on Bases, this breaks down the cohesive 'family' ties that military families enjoy by living in MQs.' She also stated that the MFRCs and other agencies would be greatly affected and that outreach programs would have to be developed to meet the needs of this spread-out customer base. Ms. Kleinschmidt stated that in her view, very little consultation with families living in MQs at present is taking place.*

If loss of our PMQs, and the subsequent change in the mandate for the MFRCs is new or upsetting to you, I strongly suggest that you make your concerns known. Since the MFNAB is representing your best wishes, they are the group that needs to voice your concerns to the decision makers. I urge all of you to use whatever means are available to you to let Ottawa know how you feel. If you don't, then the safety and comfort you feel, especially when your partner is away for long periods of time, will be gone.

It is wrong, wrong, wrong to do away with PMQs as they provide the nucleus of support especially to young families. With families moving away from base housing and integrating into the civilian community, we are changing the dynamics of our community—there no longer will be one!

We could possibly see the end of our resource centres, as we know them today—and that is unacceptable. But no one seems to be looking that far down the road. *DND just doesn't have the foresight to do enough long-range planning as far as military families are concerned.* No one seems to care—except the families.

• • •

Whatever military wives are, one thing they are *not* is "dependent." That was made very clear to me during my research for my first book, *Hurry Up and Wait.* Women resented that label tremendously because they all felt (and still do) that if anything, they are definitely 'independent.'

DND eventually got the message and stopped referring to wives as dependants. Instead the term "military spouse" began to appear here, there and everywhere. It seemed a better label since it also included the men who stayed at home while their wives pursued military careers. And so, little by little, the old made way for the new—much to the delight of military wives everywhere.

On March 17, 2003, a retired military member of Petawawa, Ontario submitted a letter to the editor of the *Pembroke Daily Observer* (Pembroke, Ontario), which caused quite a stir within the military community. Ironically it wasn't only because of his original rant, but also because he referred to me as a *dependent wife* in a rather derogatory manner. As a result of my sharing his comments with military wives across Canada and the USA, I was deluged with e-mails, and the ladies and gents were not shy in voicing their opinions. It was a good two weeks before the sizzle over the e-mail wires subsided. Not only that, but several military wives also submitted letters to the editor, some of which were published.

Mr. Brown's original complaint was over my explanation of what PMQ stood for. I had previously written an article in my weekly column in the *Pembroke Daily Observer* commending a young military couple on how they had used their wonderful decorating talents to make their PMQ their own. And, as I always do when using military abbreviations, I included an explanation of what the abbreviations represented so that my civilian readers would fully understand my writings. Mr. Brown's letter to the editor was titled "Not Taking It Any More."

Editor:

That's it! I've had it! I'm tired of people spouting off supposed military jargon and not knowing what it means, or using American military terminology and thinking that the Canadian military uses the same. For example: PMQ does not mean 'private married quarters.' They are publicly owned, not private, and are for use by all ranks, not just the privates.

PMQ doesn't mean 'permanent married quarters' (my definition) *as they aren't meant for anyone to live there permanently, but are designed for the military's mobile lifestyle. In some cases they were built because no civilian accommodation was available and at other times because unscrupulous landlords were taking advantage of military families. They sure came in handy in the early '90s when local real estate costs doubled on speculation of 1RCR moving here from London.*

And PMQ doesn't stand for, as one so ill-informed Observer *reporter once said, 'people's married quarters.' This isn't the Soviet Union. If you don't know what it means, look it up. That's what good reporters and editors are supposed to do.*

PMQ stands for personnel married quarters. Personnel. A word commonly used in the Canadian Military, i.e. married personnel, single personnel, personnel carrier, etc. Dianne Collier should know better. She was a military spouse, or dare I say, a dependent wife for many years.

Even many of those in the surrounding civilian community can't be completely forgiven. Petawawa has been a garrison town for almost 100 years, longer than all but a very few have ever lived, and countless others from all over the Ottawa Valley have worked, as civilian employees or contractors on the base.

For how many years has the Observer *published stories about the military? Yet each time I read one of the articles I picture the editor locking a reporter away in a small dark room and 'indoctrinating' him by subjecting him to days of American sitcoms such as 'Sgt Bilko,' 'McHale's Navy,' 'Gomer Pyle,' and 'Major Dad' prior to sending him off to interview base personnel. Part of the media's job is to educate the public, but you aren't doing a very good job. The least you can do is to learn Canadian military lingo....*

This letter caught me completely by surprise. As someone who tries to get along with everyone, I was taken aback at the letter's strong, angry tone. My first reaction was to ask my husband what PMQ meant—his response: Permanent Married Quarter. It's all we've ever known them to be called. But, I decided to poll my local and on-line friends (military spouses and members of the military) and I asked all of them what PMQ stood for.

What a question! I had no idea the strong feedback I would receive. Many searched Canadian Forces Administrative Orders, and Queens Regulations and Orders, and one husband even found a reference to the housing provided on military bases for military personnel in the *Chief of the Defence Staffs Annual Report of 1999 – 2000* (page 13).

After about a week of burning the e-mail and telephone lines with discussions on this issue, it was obvious that there were three definitions that people were familiar with: Permanent, Personnel and Private. The fact that several of my friends and acquaintances took the time to seek out the proper name of military housing was gratifying. Once the discussion on the definition of PMQ abated, I then shared Mr. Brown's letter to the editor with everyone, as well as all the responses I had received to my question.

I once lived in a lovely yellow PMQ surrounded by beautiful matching yellow tulips. It was a warm and comfortable home and it didn't matter to me as a newly married woman to the military lifestyle whether it stood for Personnel Married Quarters or Private Married Quarters or even People's Married Quarters. A PMQ is simply a convenient living option for sometimes transient and often isolated military families. How important is the accuracy of the expansion for the acronym if it is used correctly? The Department of National Defence (DND) website uses all three phrases when describing PMQ. If it's good enough for DND it should be adequate enough to satisfy Mr. Brown.

With regards to the correct terminology for PMQ, [Mr. Brown] showed his lack of research and understanding of military jargon. All three of the terms are used regularly.... No one term is more correct than another in reference to our home. However, I would appreciate it in the future, if you want to make reference to my home or that of my neighbours, please refer to it as an MQ—Married Quarters as has been done for the last decade!

First of all, if you check the DND website [www.dnd.ca] you will find that the Chief of the Defence Staff's Annual Report for 1999 – 2000 *(as well as several other documents), has referred to PMQs as Private Married Quarters; the SCONDVA report has referred to PMQs as Permanent Married Quarters, and the term Personnel Married Quarters can be found only in a FAQ (frequently asked questions) published by the Ombudsman's office. Since DND itself appears to use these terms interchangeably, there seems to be no wrong answer.*

Secondly, if you take a look at www.defencelink.com, the American Military website, you will not be able to find reference to PMQs as that is not what they are called. Military Housing in the US is divided into four categories: Bachelor Enlisted Housing, Enlisted Family Housing, Bachelor Officer Housing and Officer Family Housing. Nowhere are they referred to as PMQs.

Since the British also do not call them PMQs I am forced to conclude that this is a truly Canadian name for military family houses. Perhaps next time you should verify your information before chastising someone else for inaccurate information.

I'm so glad verbal diarrhea doesn't stink because I'd have to Lysol the heck out of my computer after that piece of nonsense.... Get a real issue buddy! Well I think Mr. BMOC obviously thinks he's some sort of VIP on DND jargon but what he needs are EDs to sort him out...or drag him butt-first on the back of my AVGP till he spits dirt then put him on KD 'till his fingers bleed then haul his a** to the Q who'll have him like a prom date!

[BMOC (Big Man On Campus), ED (extra duties), AVGP (Armoured Vehicle General Purpose—Grizzly, Cougar, Coyote, etc.) KD (Kitchen Duty) and Q (short for QMSI—Quarter Master Senior Instructor*) (*I like this one, we have a short form for the acronym—only in Canada you say? Ha!)] Hell I don't even think we military types know what we're saying to each other anymore (smile!). You go open yourself up a serious can of Whoop A** Dianne.

Permanent as in the place you can call home while working at the base and for the length of your posting to it. Permanent as in where you receive your mail to pay your bills, 'cause God only knows, those never stop coming in even if you are deployed!

It personally sounds to me like he is one of those people that just like to listen to themselves talk…. Like really…what difference does it make? We all know what it is or at least anyone who cares would know…and since when does being a private have anything to do with PMQs and why would he even think that?…Go get him Dianne!

Gah! What was that guy on? My Dad was in the Navy for 39 years and we lived in PMQs quite a bit. I remember asking him what PMQ meant—his words were: private married quarters. Anyway, does it really matter that much to Mr. Brown? Poor bugger must not have anything better to do than rant on word mis-usage!

It's one thing to speak out when you KNOW you're right but he was SO wrong…. I'd like to say to him better take your own advice (get the lingo right). I'm to let you know, too, Dianne that Ian says 'give him hell,' he too read the article and thinks you should set him straight.

Wow talk about making a mountain out of a molehill. I'm certainly not going to lose any sleep over what the 'P' in PMQ stands for. Are there not more important things to worry about in life? This guy has way too much time on his hands.

I am from America and I have no knowledge of the Canadian Military other than the fact that it exists. But I feel comfortable saying that certainly the misunderstanding of the use of a word such a 'private' or 'personnel' cannot possibly make an individual suffer the way 'poor' Mr. Brown has. I wish I could empathize with him, but for now he'll just have to do with a little sympathy.

So, to Mr. Brown, you might consider getting a grip on your emotions. In America the women always catch the flack for going over the top, or being on the edge—emotional wrecks is what they call us, but I can see that in Canada it is quite the opposite. Hope you decide to make your day better, and if you are waiting on someone to utilize abbreviated words properly, then you are probably going to be disappointed.

Mr. Brown—do you have a home? If yes, perhaps you could find more ways to relieve your frustration, by volunteering at a homeless shelter, instead of exerting your anger in such a rude and negative manner. Please do not be offended, you might actually be a happier person, and realize such mistakes are not as important as the other more life-threatening issues out there that you could help, even a little, to relieve. I know we all feel frustrated sometimes, but oh my goodness…. I've personally never lived in them, but I'm more concerned for my husband's safe return from Bosnia, as is he, than about the correct definition of PMQ!

On the 'dependent wife' issue:

Perhaps before slamming the editor of the Pembroke Daily Observer, *journalists, columnists and community members, Mr. Brown needs to educate himself! Welcome to the post-dependent era of the military! I have proudly been a military wife for the past 13 years. Not once during that time have I been referred to as a 'dependent wife,' as Mr. Brown dared to call Dianne Collier. Shame on you, Mr. Brown, for reversing what advocates for military wives, like Dianne, have done for us all by removing such degrading and demoralizing titles. It is thanks to the women before us that my generation of military wives enjoy a heightened awareness by the military echelons, complete with respect and honour.*

As my father always told me—smile when someone is being an idiot!

I am just like you, bouncing off the walls, how dare he! He said that PMQs were built because of bad landlords. That is not completely true. Many were built because in some locations there was not enough housing in the local communities for [military members]. He needs to be given the new name (MQ). Also, a comment on his use of the term 'dependent': I know what I would say and it wouldn't be very ladylike. How childish to have a little hissy fit and use a term (dependent wife) that we don't hear often now except from the remaining old boys' network!

As for the dependent wife wisecrack—I think the husbands might have a different view. Who handles the bills, repairs, rent, insurance, kids, etc. when your husbands are deployed? The fairy godmother? I think not!

He called you a dependent wife! I think we need to teach this man a lesson and bring him into today's world!

Please would you give this man a slap behind the head for calling you a dependant? For God's sake, we are gonna have to re-freeze this caveman!

I'm sorry you have had to deal with such a person. Family members are no longer referred to as dependants and, in fact, we in the administration/financial world (now called Resource Management types, i.e. clerks) are trained never to use this term in verbal or written forms so as not to offend anyone. I actually agree with this [rule] of my own accord. I was treated quite badly at the other end of that term when I first married and so have always taken offence at being called someone's dependant—just my youthful feminist angst I guess. Heck Dianne, a person could write an entire piece on the social impact of terminology in the Forces. The reality, however, in my mind, is that while the establishment tries to keep up with or change with the times, if we focus only on using correct terms then we will miss the boat on the issues so to speak. That's like telling a clerk that boots without a proper shine will make him or her a bad budget manager. I'm certain the entire point of your article was far more important or valuable than the fact that an older term was inadvertently used.

Dependent?? Children are dependent—spouses are equals! How dare he! Go get him Dianne.

I am a 'dependent wife' and proud of it! Label me what you will—I am confident in my worth. I come from a long line of 'sister' dependent wives who I am proud to call friend. Grrrr…go get 'em Dianne!

I am absolutely outraged! At first the whole thing about PMQs was like—what a jerk for seeing the need to address this to begin with. But as I got further down the e-mail and read his remark about Dianne being a dependent wife, that really did it for me. The fact that anyone would have those thoughts, let alone have them printed in the newspaper, is appalling! He certainly can't be married or is an utter fool for not realizing that such a statement is derogatory to military spouses and women in general! …I'm more than annoyed!

As you have no doubt gathered from the responses above, many people within the military community were quite upset at Mr. Brown's comments. I did write a response to his letter to the editor but only a toned-down version appeared in print. However, my full response did appear on my website's discussion page and part of my response included excerpts from responses I'd received from others.

I would like to share with you a few other points in my response:

When we were posted to Cornwallis in Nova Scotia, there were two types of housing for military families—TMQs and PMQs. The temporary married quarters (TMQs) were old World War II buildings converted to accommodate several families. Since Cornwallis was situated in the middle of nowhere, civilian accommodations were almost non-existant and military families were sometimes housed in TMQs while they awaited the availability of a permanent married quarter. TMQs were also available in the case of a family having to vacate their PMQ because of a fire or flood or for some other reason. As we traveled on through the years, these old WWII buildings could also be seen at other bases and I visited relatives living in them in Halifax.

As for Mr. Brown's attempt at labelling me as a dependent wife in a rather derogatory way, if he hoped by doing so that it would raise my stress level, it had the opposite effect. I just smiled as I considered the source.

Chapter 11

Life After the Military

The people are what we miss the most.

Yes—there is life after the military! For some, it means taking a complete break from the military community, where they have probably spent most of their adult lives, and moving back home—to the community they grew up in. Others will choose to remain close to the last base on which they served. And yet another group will find themselves moving to wherever a civilian job is available because living on a military pension—something we all dream we will do—is not always an option. This chapter deals with some of the trials and tribulations of adjusting to a life outside the very familiar military community.

Every time I turn around in the house, I'm bumping into him. I don't have my own space anymore and he really needs to get a life!

Being a military wife was a wonderful and dreadful occupation. The worst thing about a military marriage is that issues never seem to be resolved. Because of frequent and sometimes extended separations the practical matters (Does Jenny need braces? Will Mike play soccer? What should we do about a new car?) need to be resolved. But some of the deeper issues and conflicts are pushed to the back of the closet. Who wants to spend the time together dealing with the tough stuff? So when retirement comes, the time together to catch up, to have fun and to do restful things is wonderful. But the old habit of avoiding conflicts is no longer satisfactory and things sneak out of the closet and into the daylight. This has made for some difficult times.

However, the qualities that drew us together in the first place are still there

192

and the shared memories of all the people and places that made life so interesting are a good foundation to build on. This is said so often that it has become a cliché, but it's still so true: the people are what we miss the most. I have friends all across the country, but very few friends in my home city. So I have continued to do what I did for 30 or more years. I have formed a retirees club and worked very hard to make it a success. [I have created] a dining-out group and a bridge group. I do sewing, cross-country skiing and other sports. I join golf groups for women, Tai Chi groups, swim clubs, etc. These are all good, but never will I find the sense of community and common purpose that I felt in a military community. But the advantage is that now I don't have to save curtains in case they might fit the windows in my next house. I throw out things, secure in the knowledge that I will live in the same house for the foreseeable future.

My husband has been retired from the military now for about 10 years. Retirement has not been a holiday, since we still had two children to help with university and a house to buy. Then came a job layoff and we had to move again and away from our son and daughter-in-law. Our daughter is working in another province. I just wish our children could live closer to us. Retirement does bring some problems, in that my husband is always here, and he always wants to know what I am doing. I know he is just interested in his wife, but it is hard to get used to. As a military wife I was always used to making my own decisions and now I have to talk them over with my husband.

I also found that both my family and his family (since we now live two hours away) want us to go to everything but they are not willing to visit us and everything has to be their way. As a military wife, I did learn to handle emergencies on my own and to solve any problems on my own. I have enjoyed all the military postings and travel. As a teenager, I wanted to travel, and with the military I did get to visit the countries I was interested in and I thank God for this.

Ex-military members still feel and will always feel they are military members, whether they wear the uniform or not. It's an ingrained feeling that stays with them even after they've left the CF (they never really leave, do they?). I believe the same holds true for their spouses. Many of us entered this lifestyle at a very young and impressionable age. Many gave birth to and raised our children in this lifestyle. It's what we know best.

It's comforting to us. It will always remain with us and there's nothing wrong with that. 'If it ain't broke, don't fix it.'

The SCAN [Second Career Assistance Network] seminar is a very good seminar to attend. It does answer many post-service questions but doesn't go far enough into the stress of severing all ties with what you have known for much of your adult life. I do think that is why people become attached to their regimental associations. We women are used to finding our way in new communities but the men have a very hard time adjusting to a life without their male companions. We women have to adjust to having a man around all of the time. I think both have to learn how to become independent, living together.

Retirement! Finally I can paint my kitchen black if I want to. Having bought and sold a few homes over the years, we always went with neutral colors for painting and carpeting, etc., so that [the house] would be more appealing to a prospective buyer. I used to joke when we'd [once again] been through the emotional turmoil of selling our home by saying, 'I can't wait until we don't have to move anymore so I can paint my kitchen black.' In many ways I miss the challenge of moving and fixing up a new home and it did take a while to realize that we wouldn't be moving any more. I did worry for a bit how I would feel staying where we are for the rest of our lives, but we have been here for many, many years and it offers a lifestyle we really like. And no, I never did have a black kitchen, but at least I know that I don't have to decorate my home with someone else in mind—I can do whatever makes me happy. That's a feeling worth its weight in gold.

Retirement for me was a complete break from the military, in that my husband and I separated and then divorced. We had been together for almost twenty-five years, and all that time he was in the Army. Suddenly, I was no longer his wife, and no longer a part of the military 'family.' In many ways, leaving the military was at least as hard as leaving my husband. It was a way of life I had grown to love and feel a real part of. I live in England now, and still stay in touch with a few of my old friends from the many postings we shared. It's a funny feeling though…so many of them are still 'in,' and I'm such an outsider, at least in my own mind!

My husband retired six months ago after 25 years in. Our lives haven't changed much though as he still works at the same job except he's doing it for the ASD [Alternate Service Delivery] provider instead of the CF. The only difference is the knowledge that we will not be moving unless WE want to.

Although my husband has been retired for almost three years now, I still feel like a 'military wife' so I was really happy to find this site by accident. In a lot of ways I miss the life as much as my husband does—but I really do not miss the UN postings. Good luck to all who are still in there pitching. Remember that 'this too shall pass.'

Gary and I just bought a motorbike—what a hoot! It's like we're reliving our teenage years! Of course our kids think we've lost it and we're going through our mid-life crisis. Yep, they're right about the latter part. Ha!

Life after the military was very scary for us as my husband was medically released from the forces even though he was close to retirement age. When you have health concerns that result in your having to leave the military, you leave with a different mindset than if you retired. When you retire it's because you have either reached the age limit or have decided you want to move on to another career, another phase in your life. You make the decision. But when you are medically released, that decision is taken from you. You are basically being told that the military no longer has room for you. And for anyone that has devoted his entire adult life, or even part of it to giving his all to the military, it's quite a kick in the stomach when you are medically released.

The uncertainty, financial concerns, worry about how you are going to live and support your family can be overwhelming when you are already dealing with a serious enough illness to have required your medical release in the first place.

This medical release cloud was hanging over our heads for a long time, and when my husband's release message finally came, I was surprised by my emotions. I felt relief, not panic as I had anticipated! I worried so much for so long and hated being in limbo. But I hated more the thought of leaving our

safe, secure military life behind us. But when we knew it was going to happen, it felt as if a weight had been lifted. We were no longer in limbo; we had
a way to move forward and we did.

*The SCAN seminars are very informative but we need to have 'real'
people up there who have gone through the emotions of leaving the
Forces and dealing with civilian life. They need to tell us that 'yes, you will
feel somewhat of an alien living on civvy street. It will take you a couple of
years to settle and feel like yourself.' The realization that one does not have to
worry about picking up and moving every four years or so—this can be a
shock to your system. We will probably always have itchy feet to move on and
explore more—but it's okay to settle down and just be still. That is not always
an easy thing to do for military families.*

*Life after the military has been an adjustment. We didn't retire
where we always thought we would but are very happy with our
choice. It was more important for us to remain close to our children and their
families than it was to find an idyllic place for the two of us. Being apart
from our own families as we moved from posting to posting all those years,
we didn't want that separation from our children and grandchildren. We
wanted the complete family atmosphere we couldn't give our own children.
We have been extremely lucky to have all ended up in the same community
and we see our children and grandchildren on a regular basis. Life is good!*

If only this kind of support (the website) *was available to us during
my husband's career spanning 30 years. He was a construction engineer and I could fill a book with the memories of good times and bad. I would
not change our military life for anything and was very sad when he decided to
retire. One time he was posted to Alert, North West Territories, and our sewer
collapsed, leaving me with my family visiting from Ireland and no bathroom
facilities for two days. But we coped, for that was the military wife's way. Our
eldest son was six weeks old before his Dad was able to hold him in his arms;
he had been on course in Ontario and we were living in British Columbia.
Thank God for the support of our Navy friends there that were our family. For
those wives and sweethearts who are lonely, keep the faith and be strong.*

At first I was nervous about how we would get along living under the same roof seven days a week, as we had spent about half of each year apart when he was in the military. I was well into my own schedule and routine around the house, and I was worried about how having my husband home all day, every day was going to throw a well-laid-out routine off-kilter. Since I was still working after he retired, it was a bit easier than I thought. He took over getting the groceries and doing some of the errands I'd had to juggle on my lunch hours or on my way home from work for so many years. He also took over cooking the meals, which was a godsend. Mind you, his cooking left a lot to be desired at first. But, he's graduated from making Rice Krispie squares to making Black Forest cake, so things are improving.

There were times when we did trip over each other in the kitchen because, ironically, he suddenly looked on the kitchen as his and I was encroaching on his territory. We only had one disagreement about how to cook a meal. It was my turn to cook and hamburg was the order of the day. I'm not used to having someone look over my shoulder while I'm at the stove, and having him stirring a pot I'd just stirred two minutes before really got under my skin. But it was his commenting that he didn't cook hamburg the way I did that got to me. But I was so proud of myself. I kept my cool, and politely told him I realized he cooked it differently (without onions or mushrooms or gravy) but that I had been cooking hamburg for 50 years this way and was quite happy with how it turned out and I didn't plan on changing now. I was so pleased that he got the message, left the room and never criticized me for my cooking after that.

Life is what you make of it. Having been through all the ups and downs of this fantastic, challenging military lifestyle as well as a serious family illness, my husband and I prefer to take the humorous road. Life is just too short to do otherwise. When he came home with a Christmas gift given to him by a co-worker, little did I know that it would, in some small way, change our lives.

My husband had seen the comment on a bumper sticker attached to a passing car. The comment really hit his funny bone and so when he went back to work, he asked his co-workers to keep an eye open for this bumper sticker as he would love to have one. Much to his surprise, one of his peers had the comment made into a large sign and presented it to him at the office Christmas party. The sign read, *Gone Fishing, Dog's OK, Beware of Wife!*

When he showed me his gift, I asked him what he planned on doing with it. His reply: "Put it in the living room window of course!" As if there was no debating the issue.... But, sensing how much that sign suited him I replied, "Go for it!"

For about a year or so the sign was prominently displayed in the window and provoked many, many responses, including those of a few fishing buddies who wished that their wives would "let" them put a similar sign in their windows. After a while, I decided that the window needed to be better balanced—I needed a sign to offset his. And so the hunt was on for some comments that would, of course, top his. As we all gathered in the living room to celebrate my birthday, I opened a gift and immediately started laughing so hard I was crying. The rest of the family couldn't see what was in the box, until I held it up and showed them. On a little framed paper were the words, "Missing, husband and dog—$100 reward for the dog!" This was it! This was what I had been looking for.

Unbeknownst to my husband, I approached a good friend of his to see if he could help by making a suitable sign for me. When I told him the story, he was not only eager to help but thought it was time someone got ahead of hubby. When he asked me what size sign I would like, I said it really didn't matter—as long as it was bigger than my husband's. And it is.

Today, several years later, the signs are still hanging in the window, still bringing smiles to those who pass in front of our home and still giving us a feeling of being a "matched pair." We wouldn't have it any other way.

Chapter 12

Bloom Where You're Planted

I look upon each move as an adventure to be lived and enjoyed.
No matter how much we like where we live 'now', it can be just
as good in the next place if we have the right attitude.

What is it like packing up and moving every couple of years? For some it's a new adventure, but for others there is dread at the thoughts of pulling up stakes one more time. However, whatever your feelings are on the subject, frequent moves are a reality of military life. Military wives really do set the tone for their entire family during a move and it's their responsibility to ensure that it is a positive experience for the children. It's the wife's responsibility because sometimes she must oversee the entire move on her own, without her husband's help. Duty can keep him from accompanying his family on a move, sometimes at the last minute and in that case, his partner must assume all the responsibilities. However, these situations are few and far between.

Regardless of his family's feelings towards any particular location, a military member has to go wherever his employer sends him. Approaching any move with a positive, adventurous attitude can make the transition much easier and can help lessen the guilt the military member might feel knowing his partner is not happy about moving somewhere new. One of the biggest stress factors for any family move is a fear of the unknown. I've heard many people over the years object loudly to a posting location only to complain just as loudly a few years later when they must reluctantly, and often in tears, leave the same location. Each posting is definitely what you make of it.

The wise wife or mother will plan ahead by obtaining information about the new location that she can share with the family during the trip to their new destination. The more information the children have about the new area they will be living in, the less apprehensive they will be. Many couples take lots of photographs when they go on their house-hunting trip to the new location that they can bring home to share with the family. Just being able to see what their new home will look like can help lessen the children's apprehension.

If the new posting is not a popular one, it can seem to last 10 times as long unless you adopt a positive attitude. If you can tell yourself that you don't have to stay there forever, and try to make the most of it while you are in that location, the time will go by that much faster. You really do need to adopt an attitude of blooming where you are planted.

I've always enjoyed the challenge of a new posting. Moving is such an emotional experience—leaving friends and a good job, and not getting to see all the tulip bulbs that were planted in the garden the fall before.

Chilliwack was the best posting we ever had. Our children thrived there. We had a lovely home with a beautiful garden, lots of fruit trees, and I had the best job I've ever had. But, of course, we had to leave it all when my husband got another posting and I was devastated. I wasn't ready to leave and I couldn't even go back to our home for 'one last look' before we handed over the keys to the new owners.

It's the only posting we had that I cried my heart out about as we drove out of town. In fact, my husband clocked me and said I cried for 30 km!

There are two moving trucks on the street today. One is heading to Alberta. I am having a hard time not packing a bag and stowing away in the truck. The only thing stopping me is I don't have a porta-potty and a shower. I can't live without either and would need them for such a long haul. I have the moving itch big time watching them load.

I look upon each move as an adventure to be lived and enjoyed. No matter how much we like where we live 'now,' it can be just as good in the next place if we have the right attitude. I know that it won't be forever (only two years) this time and then we are off again. I love moving and meeting new people. It is a good thing that I'm not shy.

I know my biggest challenge was moving 'again' and leaving our only child behind. My husband and I joke that we are going through mid-life crisis together. We have found the empty nest an adjustment, for myself the most. We are in Gagetown; this was our first posting when we were newlyweds, and now we have come full circle, back again and no child.

We had two postings but they weren't typical. For the first one, we found out July 27 that we were going to England and we were there on September 1. And we did a house-hunting trip in that time as well. That was rushed. We had a very good idea that we were going but until it was official we couldn't make any financial decisions (sell the house, tell my work, etc.). We sort of knew that James was going to get a posting to Perth in October 2000, and finally got the official notice in mid-April 2002. Talk about not being able to plan, although we had a semi-official notice in December 2001. We had a lot of scrambling to do to get visas and special passports once the official posting message came through. We received our passports less than 24 hours before we had to leave. THAT was stressful!

My sister, who lives here in Edmonton, asked if we have our house listed for sale yet. I told her that we have to wait for the posting message (Joe has seen it, but it isn't in his hands yet). She replied 'It is your house—can't you do what you want? They can't tell you when to sell your own property!' I tried to explain that if we sell, and we aren't posted, we would have to pay all of the costs. She replied 'that's just dumb.'

I then tried to change the subject and she asked if I was going to go to the peace demonstration tomorrow. I told her that no matter how I feel about the war (and I didn't tell her, because I am not sure), I couldn't go. 'Why?' was the next question. How do you explain to someone like this that you could damage your husband's career? What if next week [Prime Minister] Chretien changes his mind? After I got off the phone I let out a primal scream. My sister, whom I love dearly, just doesn't get it. Civvies can't or won't understand this wonderful way of life.

We've only had two postings and they both happened in the past two years. We were very lucky that everything went smoothly and both were a great experience. Our first one came as a huge surprise. Kevin had put an OT [occupational transfer] in but it wasn't until three years later that he finally got it and the message came in. I was floored! I was so happy that he got the trade he wanted but sort of gave up on the idea because nothing had been said about it for so long.

We got our message the end of February and left for Kingston mid-April. I guess it was quick but long enough notice to get everything ready and moved without problems. That was 2001, and it was just for his course so we already knew that the following summer we would be moving again. That message seemed to take forever to come. I think because we were expecting it. Once that came through, it again was just long enough to have everything ready and we didn't feel rushed at all. What would our lives be without the wait?!

Margaret is a perfect example of a military wife who firmly believes in blooming where she is planted. Married to a Navy man, she is used to spending a lot of time apart from her husband. But, she has a very positive outlook on life and believes in enjoying as much of her surroundings as she can.

We first met on the Internet shortly before she left for a posting to England while her husband was on course there. They rented out their home and set off on another adventure. I enjoyed her e-mails very much as they were so descriptive, and she painted such a clear picture of the places she visited and events she attended that you almost felt like you were right there with her. She seemed to be continually on the go, and I admired her for making the most of her time in Britain, as I knew she was chalking up some wonderful memories.

On her return to Canada, we met when she traveled near my home to visit with a good friend. It was wonderful to meet her in person and I was even more impressed with her positive attitude and thought she was such a wonderful role model for other military wives. And, as with other women I've met over the years, I wished we lived in the same community so that our friendship could develop on a personal level instead of just through e-mails. However, it was wonderful that we had an opportunity to meet and depending on her next posting, perhaps we'll get to visit each other again.

Margaret was no sooner settled back into her home on the east coast after the family's return from Britain, than her family was moving once again (in less than a year). This move included selling their home and taking their infant daughter, who was born in England, with them—this time to Australia.

As this story is written, Margaret and her husband have spent four of the past 16 months together and her husband will be away for a total of another three months' time (not consecutive) early in the new year.

It would be ideal if, on a posting such as this, a couple would be able to travel together and share so much of a different lifestyle. Unfortunately, Margaret's husband often wasn't free to share these new experiences with her. Undaunted by this circumstance, Margaret was ensuring that she created her own memories.

During this time, she kept her communications as descriptive as before, and I often thought that having a child didn't seem to slow her down any. She was as active as she could be and her daughter, no doubt, has wonderful photo albums full of pictures that will provide wonderful memories for her in the future.

One of the things that Margaret enjoyed doing was participating in a marching band. Apparently it was quite popular in the area in which she lived, and they regularly held competitions. Like any group planning on traveling, or even those who need uniforms, they had to fundraise. In one of Margaret's messages she kept me guessing as to what fundraising event she had undertaken to help out her team. Never, in a million years would I have guessed what this enterprising young lady was up to. When I received her message below I laughed out loud and shouted, "Yesssss!" Margaret's ingenuity and willingness to do her part for the team earned her a very special nickname— one she should be extremely proud of:

I shall now tell you how we have been raising money for our team. I have raised almost $1,700 by myself. Are you curious? Be prepared to laugh at this. We (she and her friend) went to a sheep farm about 100 km away. We pulled up the floorboards of the shearing shed and our treasure was buried underneath. We shoveled sheep manure, bagged it and then sold it! The shed hadn't been cleared out for a long time so some of the manure was 17 years old. Boy oh boy, were some of the bags heavy. I weighed some of mine and they ranged from 12 to 20 kg. My daughter and I delivered more than 500 flyers in my neighborhood and we sold lots of poo at the seniors' complex just down the road from here. My team has been teasing me about the success I have had here and I am now known as the 'Sheep Shit Sheik of Shelley.

Just goes to show that no matter where you live, life is what you make of it. Shovel on Margaret!

Yes, we always bloomed where we were planted. We made the most of every posting and some we enjoyed more than others. But when we moved into our final home after retirement, I was quite apprehensive about it. What if we didn't like it there? We wouldn't be able to say, 'oh well, we'll be gone again in another couple of years.' When you are trying to deal with leaving the lifestyle for good and finally settling down in one place, it's a tremendous stressor. What if you made the wrong choice? What if you've spent your whole lifestyle in the military community—first as a dependant and then as a wife—and know no other way of life. How do you know if you can stay in one place for the rest of your life? Suddenly blooming where you are planted takes on a whole new meaning. But, having tried our best to enjoy wherever we were, we just had to hope that our planning for retirement was well done and that this next phase of our lives would still offer just as many adventures as the military lifestyle did. Besides, now I can have a real flower garden and lots of blooms that I won't have to say goodbye to.

Conclusion

In an ever-changing world, life for military spouses continues to change as well. Regardless of the challenges they face, military spouses remain committed to their partners and to the nomad lifestyle, and they should receive much more credit than they do. After all, these special people are almost single-handedly raising tomorrow's peacekeepers.

The Canadian Military establishment plays a pivotal role in the changes that military members and their families face today. Having to do more with less, trying to catch up after years and years of neglect by our government, our military members are meeting all challenges as well as they can. Some feel that we have slipped from our world position as the number one country to call on for peacekeeping duties, not because we no longer have the capability, but because we have to beg and borrow support from other countries to transport us to where we are needed. To many others, embarrassment is starting to seep in, and military families are leaving the CF way of life not because their time is up, but because they no longer believe in today's military.

If our military is to survive and prosper then our government needs to stop the downward spiral of neglect, and lead by example. Show our military the respect it deserves. It stands to reason that if our leaders respect our military then so will other Canadians. Top on my wish list is to see Canadians become as patriotic as our American counterparts. Their respect and support for their military have always been obvious. We can't say the same about ours. I hope that this book has given all who read it a better appreciation for what our military members and their families must endure in order to keep all Canadians safe.

When I look into the eyes of troops who have been on four, five or six tours, and see them glazed over—not with pride, but with a weariness and sadness—it breaks my heart. The government is asking too much of many of our troops, and I sincerely doubt that they can keep up this pace for much longer. They are suffering and their families are suffering. If the government doesn't put Canada's military at the top of the priority list, it's just a matter of time before Canada suffers as well.

Today more guys and gals joining the military are doing so not as young men and women fresh out of school, but with ready-made families and all the financial responsibilities and problems one would associate with family living. Their interest in joining the military is based more on financial gain than on the fulfillment of a lifelong ambition. In an economic climate where jobs are hard to find, the military represents a steady paycheck for some. Other young professionals are staying away from the military because it doesn't pay well enough. And with the recent loss of our soldiers in Afghanistan, many young men and women are re-thinking joining the military and are choosing another direction for their lives. We are certainly living in very difficult recruitment times.

Women joining the military are going on overseas tours, leaving partners and children behind. Mom is no longer the one stable force in children's lives. In fact, some children with both parents in the military have had to learn early on not only to take on the latchkey lifestyle, but also to cope without one parent, or sometimes both, for six months or more at a time.

Military wives are slowly coming out of their supportive shell. Many are no longer hesitant to voice their opinions on lifestyle or military issues. And, in addition to sharing their thoughts and concerns with their peers, they are also speaking out *to* the military when they are able, and if not, to the media out of frustration. They understand their partners' requirement to follow the chain of command, and so the spouses are speaking out because their partners can't—particularly on issues that they feel directly affect them and their families.

As this book goes to print, two military wives on different bases have gone public with their concerns over exorbitant PMQ rental rates, substandard or non-existent repairs, and unsafe and outdated military equipment. I admire their willingness to stand up and be heard, and I predict that in the future, we will see a definite increase in the number of wives who do not accept "what is" but consistently question "why" and push for answers. The genie is out of the bottle and she won't go back in.

It seems as time goes on it gets even harder for the spouses. We live in a time when the expectations of the troops and their families are higher than ever. With a generation of better-educated and 'computer literate' soldiers and families who frankly have lived a bit more of a spoiled life than you or I, it's even harder for some to adjust. Doesn't help of course that there seem to be more bullets flying in the regions we are now deploying to than in those areas we worked in in the '50s, '60s, '70s and '80s. Peacekeeping, as we like to call it, has become more dangerous than ever and certainly this is felt very strongly on the home front.

Some feel that the military is doing too much for our families and that the families' needs are growing. The system is teaching our families to depend on it and not on themselves. The results of this constant hand-holding won't be known for 20 years or more down the road when these families leave the system and must face managing on their own. They will then leave the security of this lifestyle behind them and move into the scary unknown. Will they be ready for it? Many don't think so.

I asked an e-mail group of military wives for a yes or no answer to the question of whether DND was doing enough to support the families. I was shocked to find the majority answered, *No.* Today's young military families have come into the military community with all the support networks in place—they know no other way. However, I come from a time when there were no support networks for young military wives. You depended on yourself and your friends. While I am very happy to see more support for our families, I think DND needs to take a hard look at the support offered and decide where to draw the line. When is enough enough?

Our Military Family Resource Centres are about to enter a crisis phase because they spend 90 percent of their time on 10 percent of the population. Unless the trend to tear down or sell our PMQs (place of residence for the 10 percent) changes, those who enjoy all the MFRCs have to offer will disappear into the fog of civilian living accommodations and the MFRCs' reason for being will no longer exist.

Ultimately, the loss of PMQs will mean that our military community will cease to exist. Many feel we will all be strangers working for a company—one that doesn't necessarily look out for our best interests, a company that doesn't provide the same supportive atmosphere we have all come to depend on.

Apart and aside from all the changes one finds in today's military community, the role of the military spouse remains the same—supportive. And so, military spouses are called upon now, more than ever, to rise to today's challenges. Will they? There is no doubt in my mind—it's what they do best.

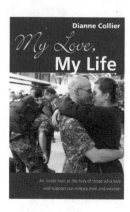

We hope you have enjoyed
My Love, My Life:
An inside look at the lives of those who love and support our military men and women
Dianne Collier
ISBN 0-921165-83-8 • $23.95 CAN $19.95 US

To order additional copies of **My Love, My Life**, please call Creative Bound Inc. at 1-800-287-8610 (toll-free, North America) or (613) 831-3641, or visit the book's website at www.mylovemylife.ca.

Other select titles by Creative Bound:

Vitamin "C" for Couples: Seven "C"s for a Healthy Relationship
Luke De Sadeleer

ISBN 0-921165-68-4
$18.95 CAN $15.95 US

Just as Vitamin C bolsters our immune system, a regular dose of (the Couples Coach®) Luke De Sadeleer's Seven "C"s will bring you closer to your partner and keep your loving relationship strong and secure.

Laughter, Love & Limits: Parenting for Life
Dr. Maggie Mamen

ISBN 0-921165-54-4
$20.95 CAN $17.95 US

From the extraordinary to the everyday— an upbeat prescription for the complications of family life.

That Perception Thing!
Dawn Brown

ISBN 0-921165-76-5
$16.95 CAN $13.95 US

Today's climate is laced with uncertainty and fear. Brown's message is simple and effective: while we can't always change the events in our lives, we can choose to change our perceptions of these events.

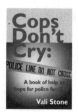

Cops Don't Cry: A book of help and hope for police families
Vali Stone

ISBN 0-921165-62-5
$20.95 CAN $17.95 US

Spouses agree that law enforcement officers grapple with real-life horrors and that the bitter belief that 'cops don't cry' is sadly untrue.

Call us today at 1-800-287-8610 to order, or visit our website at www.creativebound.com. Associations or groups, institutions, businesses and retailers—ask about our wholesale discounts for multiple-copy orders.

Bringing expertise to you!
www.creativebound.com